As someone who knows Erin personally, I can tell you that she is the real deal! Her compassionate spirit and resilient attitude shine through the pages of this book. If you are struggling financially, Erin's story will give you practical ideas to break free from barely surviving and give you hope that you, too, can go from financial frustration to financial freedom!

CRYSTAL PAINE, *New York Times* bestselling author and creator of MoneySavingMom.com

Recounting her own family's hidden struggle with poverty, Erin's story is both thought-provoking and inspiring. Filled with brutal honesty and a much-needed perspective, *More Than Just Making It* offers practical tips and real-life advice for even the most difficult of circumstances, as well as a firsthand look at the reality of the working poor in America.

RUTH SOUKUP, *New York Times* bestselling author of *Living Well, Spending Less: 12 Secrets of the Good Life*

As an everyday wife, mom, and homemaker who is just trying to live and steward my time and finances well, I so appreciated *More Than Just Making It*. Financial stuff is just hard sometimes, and trusting God in the midst of it can be confusing and painstaking. But Erin shares her story with such vulnerability and offers us all a beautiful, important, honest, practical offering, an offering that gives fresh inspiration for those weary and ready to trust more deeply. My prayer for you as you read this book is that God would "sing" to you, as Erin says, in ways you wouldn't have been able to hear otherwise.

SARAH MAE, author of *Desperate: Hope for the Mom Who Needs to Breathe* ❧

Practical and encouraging for anyone who's ever been hard up—for cash or for hope.

ANNE BOGEL, author of *Reading People: How Seeing the World through the Lens of Personality Changes Everything* and creator of ModernMrsDarcy.com

Erin has a gift of using her vulnerability for the greater good of us all. This book is a trail guide to lead us toward richer, fuller lives by living within our means with grace and grit. I'm grateful she's sharing her story with all of us.

TSH OXENREIDER, author of *At Home in the World*

More Than Just Making It shatters the stigma of what poverty looks like in America and provides the perfect mix of motivation and encouragement to help readers rise above their own financial hardships.

JESSI FEARON, financial coach and creator of Real Life Money Plan™

More Than Just Making It touches on truths that need to be discussed. It gives practical step-by-step help on how to move from financially frustrated to financially strong and sound. You will love Erin's honesty, her encouragement, and her wisdom from her journey!

ALLI WORTHINGTON, author of *Fierce Faith: A Woman's Guide to Fighting Fear, Wrestling Worry, and Overcoming Anxiety*

I love this book! Erin draws the reader into her story—not because it's perfect, but because it's not. She offers practical advice and creative solutions that the financially frustrated reader will find helpful. But it's her *be content with what we have* message that leads us into gratitude, and I love that!

KRISTEN WELCH, bestselling author of *Raising Grateful Kids in An Entitled World*

More Than Just Making It contains gems of practical wisdom you can use to turn your financial situation around, yet Erin doesn't come off sounding like some distant, know-it-all expert. Instead she vulnerably shares, in heart-wrenching detail, the specifics of her family's own financial disaster and recovery, all the while challenging the stereotypes we may unknowingly hold about the working poor.

JAMIE C. MARTIN, author of *Give Your Child the World* and cofounder of SimpleHomeschool.net

Step one to overcoming financial frustration: read this book. Step two: learn from the best and apply everything Erin suggests. *More Than Just Making It* has specific strategies to help you become financially successful. Taking immediate action on Erin Odom's advice will get you there.

VICKY LASHENKO, speaker and host of Mompreneur Show

More Than Just Making It is more than just a book about conquering your budget or establishing wise spending habits; it's more than a compassionate lifeline for the person drowning in debt. It is a journey into the heart of a loving God who wants to give you hope and a future.

EMILY WIERENGA, author of *Atlas Girl* and creator of TheLuluTree.com

Full of practical steps to climb your way out of a financial fog, *More Than Just Making It* takes a hard topic and brings it to life with authentic, relatable stories and eye-opening reflections. Erin has been there, done that and doesn't want us to do the same!

RUTH SCHWENK, coauthor of *For Better or For Kids* and creator of TheBetterMom.com and FortheFamily.org

I've read plenty of books, but few are as relatable, encouraging, and real as *More Than Just Making It*. From the very first chapter, Erin openly shares her heart, her pride, and her humility as she and her husband struggle with their financial situation. Whether you face financial crises and are looking for practical help without condemnation or need your heart softened towards those who are struggling financially, this grace-filled book is one every family should read.

TIFFANY TERCZAK, creator of DontWastetheCrumbs.com and GroceryBudgetBootcamp.com

This book is full of practical, no nonsense help for getting out of the income-problem cycle. By the time you're done reading, you'll feel like Erin is your best friend and cheerleader, holding your hand the whole way.

STACY MYERS, creator of HumorousHomemaking.com

This is a book for everyone who has ever felt hopeless or discouraged or frustrated when faced with too much month and not enough money. Erin Odom's *More Than Just Making It* is a lifeline. The book is full of practical ideas and tips—from planning your meals to second-hand shopping to ideas for creating additional income. It brings hope and speaks to the heart of learning to live with less and recognizing that even at the end of the darkest tunnel—there's always Light.

KARIANNE WOOD, author of *So Close to Amazing* and creator of ThistleWoodFarms.com

Not just another money book! A gripping story that opened my eyes to who "the poor" are, how to help them, and what financial stewardship looks like. The church needs this book.

JESSICA SMARTT, creator of SmartterEachDay.com

Erin has given us the gift of identifying with us in our times of financial stress. She is candid, sincere, relatable, and inspiring! *More Than Just Making It* is a poignant story of God's grace and provision, but it is also empoweringly practical. If you are in a season of financial struggle, this book provides a gentle squeeze to remind you that you're not alone and welcome guidance as you take steps forward in faith.

KATIE BENNETT, creator of EmbracingaSimplerLife.com

In a world that prizes financial success above all, this book gently reminds us that the posture of our hearts is more important than the dollars in our bank account. Not only is this compellingly demonstrated in the author's personal story, but the reader is offered a lifeline of hope into a better future with hard work and outside-the-box, practical ideas. This book is a gem for anyone who's ever struggled with money and offers the rare combination of practical advice with encouragement for the heart. A must-read.

BETH RICCI, creator of RedandHoney.com

Should you order this book? YES! I can assure you that whether you are barely making ends meet, find yourself continually going over budget, or are trying to find a way to finally save, this book is for YOU! Erin not only shares her story of financial frustration and her faith in God's provision, but she gives us practical steps we can take to break free from the anxiety of financial stress and make progress toward being better stewards while learning how to build a more secure future.

KELLY SMITH, author of *Everyday Grain-Free Baking* and creator of TheNourishingHome.com

Erin Odom tackles the sensitive topic of financial hardship with transparency, grace, truth, and hope. She conveys her hardships with humility, confessing she had much to learn through the challenges of an insufficient income as opposed to a spending problem. *More Than Just Making It* portrays a realistic, unpredictable, unwanted journey of financial hardship along with biblical wisdom and practical application steps for finding your way through it.

ELISA PULLIAM, life coach, author, and ministry leader at MoretoBe.com

I felt Erin's warmth, humility, and graciousness exuding from every page. I loved the blend of personal stories with Scripture and practical tips. *More Than Just Making It* is the story of how God is redeeming painful years of Erin's life into something that can be such an encouragement and so practically helpful for others. I am so excited for this book to be out in the world!

MEGAN TIETZ, coauthor of *Spirit-Led Parenting* and creator of SortaCrunchy.net and the *Sorta Awesome* podcast

More Than Just Making It offers a breath of fresh air and encouragement for anyone struggling with the financial stresses that are common but rarely talked about in today's culture. Readers will not only take comfort that they're not alone in the continual struggle to balance a family budget, but learn how to approach spending in a healthier, intentional, and more liberating way.

JESSICA KASTNER, author of *Hiding from the Kids in My Prayer Closet*

The perfect blend of real-life experience and practical tips, *More Than Just Making It* is a beacon of hope for anyone feeling overwhelmed by their financial situation. As Erin told her story, I found myself nodding along in understanding, then becoming inspired to make changes in the way we handle finances. Erin speaks with the humility and wisdom that comes from experience, making this book a relatable, encouraging, and immensely valuable resource.

KAYSE PRATT, creator of IntentionalMoms.com
and The Organized Life Planner

More Than Just Making It is more than a story of one family's financial struggle; it's an invitation for readers to come face-to-face with their pride and prejudice regarding poverty—and to come face-to-face with a very real and very present God who cares. Erin Odom is a masterful storyteller. From biblical application to practical help, Odom stewards her story beautifully for the benefit of those who are presently struggling.

WENDY SPEAKE, coauthor of *Triggers: Exchanging Parent's Angry Reactions for Gentle Biblical Responses*

Reading this book made me feel like I'm not alone. If you, too, need to be reminded that startling beauty can come out of seemingly dead-end hardship, read *More Than Just Making It*. Erin's book is eye-opening, empowering, and ultimately, an invitation to hope.

ELSIE CALLENDER, author of *Your Simple Home Handbook*
and creator of RichlyRooted.com

This isn't merely a book to help you with your finances, it's a book to help you change your perspective on finances and what it means to "make it" in our society. I never thought a book on money and finances could suck me in so completely. I am so thankful that Erin chose to share her heart and her story!

JAMI BALMET, creator of YoungWifesGuide.com

MORE

THAN JUST MAKING IT

Hope for the Heart of the Financially Frustrated

ERIN ODOM

THE HUMBLED HOMEMAKER

ZONDERVAN®

ZONDERVAN

More Than Just Making It
Copyright © 2017 by Erin Odom

Requests for information should be addressed to:
Zondervan, *3900 Sparks Dr. SE, Grand Rapids, Michigan 49546*

ISBN 978-0-310-34888-7 (softcover)

ISBN 978-0-310-35082-8 (audio)

ISBN 978-0-310-34953-2 (ebook)

Published in association with William K Jensen Literary Agency, 119 Bampton Court, Eugene, Oregon 97404.

Cover design: James W. Hall IV
Cover photography: PhotoAlto/Laurence Mouton/Getty Images®/icemanj/Shutterstock
Interior design: Kait Lamphere

First printing July 2017 / Printed in the United States of America

TO WILL AND OUR FOUR CHILDREN: We've gone from barely surviving to more than just making it together. You're the reason that I write.

IN MEMORY OF GRANNY: Although you didn't have much, your home was always filled with Hershey's Kisses and toys you had scored while thrifting, and my childhood Christmases were spent unwrapping secondhand gifts you had purchased with love. Your entrepreneurial spirit and creative ways of going from barely surviving to more than just making it live on.

CONTENTS

ONE

WHEN YOUR ECONOMY CRUMBLES

"The Lord makes poor and makes rich;
he brings low and he exalts.
He raises up the poor from the dust;
he lifts the needy from the ash heap
to make them sit with princes
and inherit a seat of honor.
For the pillars of the earth are the Lord's,
and on them he has set the world."

1 SAMUEL 2:7–8 (esv)

FALL 2010

It was a place I never imagined I would visit.

As I exited my mother's minivan, I zipped my coat and shivered, more from nerves than from the elements.

"Do you want to come inside with me?" I asked my mom.

"No, I'll just stay with the girls," she said.

I looked at my toddler and newborn and realized they would be more comfortable in the heated van with my mother. But my immediate thought was that my mom must be embarrassed. What if someone were to recognize me, were to recognize *her*, were to recognize me as *her* daughter?

"Don't forget that Judy Cook works there," she reminded me.

I made a mental note to be on the lookout for Mrs. Cook, a member of my parents' church, and to find a corner to hide in if she looked in my direction. As I entered the cold brick building, I thought the people around me looked poor and disheveled. I felt overdressed and over-groomed. I sank into the hard-backed chair in the waiting area and watched the clock. I jumped inside each time the receptionist called a name.

Please, please, don't let them say my name loudly, I prayed. I had spent much of my childhood in this community, and I was terrified that someone from my past would notice me. Thankfully, the receptionist didn't draw much attention when she called my name. She ushered me down a narrow hallway. Sure enough, I spotted Mrs. Cook in my periphery. On one hand, perhaps she'd have mercy on me if she were my case worker. On the other hand, I didn't want her or her daughter—who was my age—to know I had fallen on hard times. I didn't see it then—the pride, the condescending attitude I harbored toward those in my position.

When the receptionist passed Mrs. Cook's office and took me instead to the next one, I exhaled deeply. At least I'd be dealing with a stranger.

The case worker sat behind a desk filled with papers. She motioned for me to take a seat in front of her, and I removed my coat and sat down. She was a tall, thin African-American woman with a beautiful smile and an office filled with family photos. *She must be a mother herself*, I thought.

I wondered what she thought of me: *Did she hold any prejudices? Would she fault me for asking for help? Or would she have compassion?* I smoothed my black pinstripe pants and fidgeted with my teal wool pea coat, which lay across my lap.

"And why are you here today, Mrs. Odom?" she asked.

I smiled and feigned confidence as I began to tell our story. All the while, I wanted to scream from the rooftops that I shouldn't be there at all. That I was an educated woman. That I'd always paid my taxes and been a straight-A student in school—the valedictorian of my high school class and named "Most Outstanding Female Graduate" at my college graduation. That I was a hard worker. That I wasn't a lazy bum. That I was above the stereotypes. That I was above *this*.

None of it mattered. So instead, I told the truth.

"I'm here to apply for food stamps."

THE CRUMBLING OF PRIDE

Walking into the Department of Social Services that day was one of the most humbling events of my life. It also spotlights the condition of my character at that time. It wasn't my parents who instilled such pride in me, though. They both grew up in large families with little extra money, and although my dad's income always provided us with plenty, they practiced frugality. We didn't take elaborate vacations, wear name-brand clothing, or drive new cars. It turned out the simple lifestyle in which they had raised me would serve my family well as we navigated the murky economic landscape in the aftermath of the Great Recession.

Still, growing up in upper-middle class suburban America, we were the givers and never the recipients of charity. I was educated in private schools from kindergarten through college. I never wanted for anything. We didn't ask for help, and we would have never dreamed of using government aid. My misinformed belief was that most aid recipients were lazy, didn't work, and stole from those who had more money. *It wasn't free help, after all. It was the taxpayers' money! Someone was paying for it.* Using government services was something "good Christian families" in the South just did *not* do. And if they did, they surely didn't admit it to anyone.

The culture in which I'd spent my first three decades was that of the "haves" and the "have nots." At my Christian high school, in my private university's classes, at various churches I visited, discussions about the poor would often center around a token food or clothing drive during the holidays. Even these came with judgments.

DESPERATE TIMES CALL FOR DESPERATE MEASURES

On that humbling day back in 2010, we were in the middle of a recession that was turning our country upside down. One year earlier, my husband and I had both lost our jobs. We had a daughter who had just turned a year old, and we owned a house out of state that we couldn't sell. We now owed more on it than it was worth. My husband, Will, was working as a public school teacher in North Carolina, a state whose teachers were at the bottom of the national pay range.[1] We had more month than money.

I didn't realize *how* much we were struggling until I read a blog post[2] about a woman who was feeding her family on a food stamps budget as an experiment to prove that those on food stamps could eat well. At the time, I had no idea what income level dictated whether someone was poor or rich. My parents had never revealed their exact income to me, and they'd taught me never to ask anyone how much money they made.

A friend from church who knew of our struggle had recommended the post to me. When she told me the blogger's family was eating healthy on a food stamp budget, I couldn't wait to read all about it. Surely a food stamp budget must be close to what we paid for food—between $200 and $250 a month for our family of four. Our groceries consisted of the basics because that was what stretched our dollars—rice, beans, a little meat, and canned produce. I would walk by the organic foods in the store and look longingly at the price tags before moving on, wishing we could afford to feed our family better. I was stunned when I realized this blogger's "food stamp" budget was $600 a month for a family the same size as ours.

Boy, what I could do with a $600 monthly food budget! It seemed unreal. We'd feel rich! Our bellies wouldn't rumble at the end of the month. We could even buy organic. I'd make every inch of those stamps stretch, and we'd eat like royalty!

That blog post prompted my visit to the food stamps office. We needed more food; I saw no other way.

PRIDE COMES BEFORE THE FALL

As the case worker stared at me from behind her desk, I opened a manila envelope and gingerly pulled out our documents. I unfolded copies of our driver's licenses, our lease, my husband's pay stubs, and my last three months' checks from the newspaper where I was freelancing. I smoothed out the creases and stacked the papers neatly, as if a better presentation of our situation might salvage some dignity and convince the case worker that we were, indeed, in need of aid.

As she began examining my paychecks, I spoke up: "I'm getting paid ten cents per word to write feature stories. My income varies greatly."

"I see," she mused, as she skimmed the documentation and began typing notes on her computer keyboard. I couldn't read her, and it made me nervous.

I guess she doesn't want to get my hopes up, I thought. I sat on the edge of my chair, twisted the rings on my fingers, and looked out the window. *Can she see through me?* I wondered. *Read my inward battle?*

"One month I might make as much as $200, but another month might be only $40 or $50," I went on. "I'm always on the lookout for story ideas, though, to pitch to my editor."

I wanted her to know that I was a hard worker. But I also wanted to stay home with our babies. Although it didn't pay much, my newspaper job was allowing me to work from home.

"You see, ma'am, if I were to go out and get a full-time job as a reporter, which is the only job I'm really qualified for with my journalism degree, it wouldn't even cover the cost of daycare."

I felt I needed to justify why I was staying at home. *Perhaps I was talking too much. I always said too much.*

"Well, the computer makes the final decision," the woman explained. "I'll input all of your information, and if you need help based on these numbers, you'll qualify."

As I watched her review our documents, I realized I was no longer sure of my desired outcome. I wanted us to qualify so we could eat better and didn't have to look at a bare pantry and refrigerator at the end of the month and so I could give my toddler an extra apple if she asked for one. At the same time, I hoped we still made enough money that we wouldn't qualify—that I could say we'd never "taken advantage" of the system.

I didn't see my pride at the time, never noticed that I'd neatly divided society into two groups: "us" and "them." People like *us* were generous in giving to the poor. The Bible was clear that we were to take care of the less fortunate. So we collected canned goods, hygiene supplies, and gently used clothing, and gave to soup kitchens and the local Christian mission.

At age fifteen, I'd publicly declared that God was calling me to be a missionary—most likely to Latin America. I'd gone on mission trips to urban American cities as well as to developing countries. I'd witnessed poverty as an outsider, but I'd never lived it. While in the slums of Peru during my early twenties, I wrote in my journal, "People in the US are taught to dream dreams and make goals and reach for the stars. People here are just surviving from day to day. They are *just barely making it.*"

But as for those in my own city, in my own town? I never looked them in the eyes, never considered that people with whom I brushed shoulders at the grocery store or walked past on the streets could be struggling as well, could be crushed with the weight of not having enough money to feed their children, of not being able to go to the doctor, of not having sufficient funds to pay the next month's rent. I said I loved the poor, but I really just pitied them. I never got to know them or their stories. I made assumptions. I never stopped to wonder how they got there or gave a thought to how the cycle of poverty could be stopped.

It would take walking among the impoverished in my own city, listening to their stories, changing my preconceived notions, and experiencing my own humbling circumstances for those living on a low income to become real to me.

TWO

AND IT ALL COMES
TUMBLING DOWN

The disappointments that strangle us today will soon be forgotten.

ANGIE SMITH, *SEAMLESS*

JULY 2009
Vancouver, British Columbia

The airplane shook as it ascended, but I was too fatigued to care. I sat next to my husband, the one I couldn't live without but who felt like the enemy at that moment. A few minutes later, our bubbly toddler stood in her seat and began playing with the hair of the person in front of us. I didn't notice until the flight attendant stopped at our aisle and asked if she could take our little girl for a walk around the plane.

"Would you, please?" *Was I really asking a stranger to take my child off my hands?*

She smiled and said it would be her pleasure. Maybe she didn't want to cause a fuss with those who had surely complained about our daughter. Perhaps she saw my swollen eyes, my tear-streaked cheeks.

We were supposed to be en route to the destination of our dreams. Instead, we were flying home. I'd been up all night and had slept fitfully the entire week, cleaning the tiny one-bedroom apartment—scrubbing the toilets and floors, dusting, vacuuming—as if I could scour away the pain.

As the flight attendant took our daughter, I lifted the window shade to catch one last glimpse of the mountains. The clouds covered them.

ONE WEEK EARLIER

My fraying, deep blue leather Bible lay open on my lap. It was the NIV *Student Bible* my parents had given me for high school graduation ten years earlier; the one that had traveled with me to Puerto Rico, Peru, Argentina, Costa Rica, China, and Zimbabwe; the one that held so many scribbles of promises and prayers. I sat on the balcony porch of our apartment, looked up at the majestic, snow-capped Vancouver mountains, and read from James 1:2–8 (NIV 1984):

> Consider it pure joy, my brothers, whenever you face trials of many kinds, because you know that the testing of your faith develops perseverance. Perseverance must finish its work so that you may be mature and complete, not lacking anything. If any of you lacks wisdom, he should ask God, who gives generously to all without finding fault, and it will be given to him. But when he asks, he must believe and not doubt, because he who doubts is like a wave of the sea, blown and tossed by the wind. That man should not think he will receive anything from the Lord; he is a double-minded man, unstable in all he does.

It was July, but a damp chill hung in the air. I sipped my coffee and pulled a blanket up around my shoulders. *Why have you taken me here today, Lord?* I whispered.

Trials. I thought back to my mom's cancer when I was seventeen and its return when I was twenty-one, then to my friend's instant death in a car accident when I was a freshman in college—undoubtedly two of the most traumatic challenges I'd experienced to date. My mind wandered back to the six months during which we had tried and failed to sell our little starter home in Mississippi. That felt like a trial for sure, but even though the rules said we had to sell our house before leaving for the mission field, the agency had granted us an exception, as long as we rented it out.

Life is good now, Lord, I whispered. *Life is good. Why are you taking me here?* My heart turned over and fell into my stomach. *It's been a while since I've experienced a real trial, Lord. What lies ahead?*

We were parents to a beautiful little girl, and our dream of becoming missionaries was coming true. We had been living in stunning Vancouver for nearly four months, working with Hispanic immigrants and participating in missionary training courses. Soon we would be leaving for our final destination, Mexico.

We had high hopes for the path ahead, but we were also struggling in our marriage. Living far away from our strong support network heightened tensions we'd been battling for years. When Will's parents announced their divorce after thirty-eight years of marriage, he chose to reveal some personal struggles that sent our own marriage into an even deeper tailspin. We confessed our marital hardships to our missions agency, and they rightly asked us to leave. We were devastated, but there was nothing else to be done. We hurriedly packed up our apartment and prepared to head home to my parents in North Carolina instead of to Mexico.

STARTING OVER

We arrived in Charlotte with next to nothing: two bags each, a Pack 'n Play, a stroller, and each other. My parents awaited us at the airport. There were no "Welcome Home" posters, no balloons, no celebration. A palpable sadness seemed to hang over the baggage claim. Despite the circumstances, however, my parents offered their love, support, and even their home to us.

Their firstborn daughter—the one who'd always pursued and succeeded at excellence—had been on the cusp of achieving her lifelong dream of becoming a missionary. Now she was falling apart. Our pastors and counselors advised us to settle our family in North Carolina, where my parents could help us slowly begin the process of rebuilding our lives. My pregnant sister and her husband were already living with my parents in their three-bedroom home, yet they made space for our little family as well.

We had no jobs, no car, a meager savings, a daughter to feed, and a home in another state that we hadn't been able to sell. *At least we have renters*, we told ourselves. *We'll keep renting it out until we can sell it.*

I had sensed the Lord warning me of a trial to come. *Why, Lord?* I asked. *Could God make something beautiful out of this? Our dreams for the mission field were shattered, but could He breathe life back into our marriage? And if so, when? How soon? Would we spiral in this darkness forever?*

I spent much of the next six weeks in my younger brother's childhood room. Our family of three shared the smallest space in the house. The full bed took up most of the floor, an old sewing table turned computer desk was wedged beneath one window, and another window on the adjacent wall allowed sunlight to wake me each morning. Most days, I pulled the covers over my face and drifted back into unconsciousness until ten o'clock, while my sister or mom took our daughter and diapered, clothed, fed, and played with her as I battled my thoughts and emotions.

My once-full spirit felt only emptiness, and despite my lack of appetite, I gained ten pounds within the first two weeks. That's what Mama's cooking does, even a decade after leaving home. Still, nothing filled me—no amount of food or Bible reading or prayer. Fatigue consumed me, and although my spirit felt split into a million pieces, no tears flowed.

While I slept or read books on forgiveness and healing, Will searched job postings. Miraculously, he had five interviews and three job offers within that first week. They were all low-paying teaching positions, but they were jobs nonetheless.

Few people knew of the circumstances under which we had left Canada—that our marriage was barely hanging on by a thread. We were supposed to be a missionary couple: strong, united, and ready to fulfill God's work in the world. The reality weighed me down with shame. Every time I left my parents' home or logged in to Facebook, it felt like the entire world was looking at me, as if people could see my empty, wounded heart.

Little did we know that our marriage problems would pave the way for financial hardship to define our next four years, that the home we'd left behind would continue losing value, that my husband's teacher salary would leave us with little to live on, that we'd experience medical emergencies and surprise pregnancies, that we'd have to survive on government aid. We would hold onto the only things we had—God and each other.

FINDING HOME

While my parents were gracious to host us, we never intended to stay with them long-term. As soon as Will secured a job teaching high school Spanish, we began looking for an apartment or rental home on Craigslist. On Will's salary our options would be limited. Still, we hoped to find somewhere safe and comfortable. The listing for 136 Kayley Circle drew me in immediately: a two-bedroom, two-story townhouse would more than meet our needs compared to the tiny one-bedroom apartment we'd leased in Vancouver. But the monthly payment would leave us with barely enough money to cover food, utilities, and unforeseen expenses. However, after spending hours scrolling through rental listings, it became clear we'd be hard-pressed to find anything else to fit our budget.

I emailed the landlord to schedule a showing, mentioning that I admired her writing style and how inviting she'd made the townhouse sound in her description. She wrote back that she was an English teacher, and writing was her passion. I replied that writing was a passion of mine as well—one I'd let go but hoped to revive soon—and that my husband was also a teacher. Unbeknownst to me, this casual exchange was paving the way for the rental we'd call home for the next four years.

When we met to tour the townhouse, I wasn't surprised that the landlord's smile was as warm as her writing style. Just as she'd described, the home was lovely. At the end of the showing, we shook hands and parted ways. As soon as we hopped back into my mom's Dodge Caravan, I looked at Will and said, "Can we please rent it? I love it! I don't think we'll find anything cheaper with this much room. And it's only twenty minutes away from your job."

Will agreed that the townhouse was our best option, but how could we swing the payment? Would we be able to make it? Could we justify such an expense?

I wrote the landlord one last email:

Hi Jenny,

Thanks so much for showing us the home today. Your Craigslist description, though elegant, was no exaggeration. The house is gorgeous, and the neighborhood would be a safe and welcoming place for us to call home. I hate to ask this, but is the price firm? If there is any wiggle room, would you be willing to lower the rent by fifty dollars a month?

Warmly,
Erin

To my utter shock, she wrote back almost immediately.

Dear Erin,

Your family charmed me from the moment we met. Your little redheaded daughter is a delight, and after we finished the tour, I called my husband and told him we'd found the perfect tenants, even mentioning that I'd be willing to lower the price if you were interested. The house is yours.

Sincerely,
Jenny

And just like that, we had a place to live. I became a Craigslist scout, and we purchased secondhand nearly everything we needed for our home. Just as we'd negotiated our rent, I bargained to knock down the price of furniture. College friends gave us a bedroom suite, and a truck driver friend from Mississippi volunteered to bring us the few furnishings we still owned. It was not the place we'd thought we'd be spending the next year, and the future was still uncertain. Even so, we thanked the Lord for providing for our needs and set out to establish our new home. We hoped it would be temporary, but the walls of the townhouse would witness our financial crisis unfolding over the next four years.

A RECESSION OF THE HEART

Our financial hardships were a perfect storm: the effects of poor decisions from our newlywed days, marriage trials that had led to job loss, and a nationwide recession. Moving to a new state isolated us from our friends except through social media, and every time we logged in to Facebook, we saw joyful status updates of new homes, Disney World vacations, and pregnancies. Our world was shrouded in depressing circumstances while our colleagues and friends were living in bliss, or so we thought. We were ashamed to tell anyone we were struggling. We didn't understand we were part of a whole generation living under financial duress.[1]

While our marriage difficulties initiated our descent into financial frustration, for others it is excessive spending, unforeseen medical emergencies, costly home repairs, job loss, or student loans. In the mid-2000s, those born in the 1980s were just starting their families. Many were steeped in student loan and credit card debt. As job markets began to decline, many faced low-paying jobs or no work at all. Even those in high-paying careers were crushed with the weight of paying for the education that got them those jobs in the first place. Then, in late 2007, the Great Recession hit.[2]

The economic downturn made our financial difficulties seem

insurmountable, and we struggled to hold onto any shred of hope in the aftermath of our cross-country move and in our floundering marriage. We *thought* we'd done everything right. Will and I both graduated from college with honors. He obtained his master's degree directly afterward. We purchased a home for much less than what the bank said we could afford. But none of that mattered now.

Even though we'd bought a home below our means in 2006, by 2009 the national mortgage crisis had led to our mortgage—along with millions of others'—being underwater.[3]

The recession had prompted many school systems, like Will's, to institute a salary freeze that lasted several years. The price of food,[4] gas,[5] and other basic necessities[6] continued to rise while income levels stagnated. Our experience taught me that many Americans—regardless of the current economy—are often just one paycheck away from financial ruin.[7] In fact, although the Great Recession officially ended in June 2009,[8] a 2015 report showed that 70 percent of American families were still experiencing financial frustration because of low incomes, lack of savings, or debt.[9] While the economy has improved overall, not everyone has recovered.

Although these facts may be disheartening, I'm here to encourage you. Regardless of your financial situation, there *is* hope. While this book will chronicle our family's journey through our most hopeless financial season, it will also show you how we broke free of the cycle of financial frustration and made a comeback.

Perhaps your family is barely making ends meet on a low income, like mine was. Maybe the IRS says you are middle or upper income, but your debt note shows otherwise; credit card companies and student loans have a chokehold on you, and you don't know how to break free. Or it could be that you feel hopeless in other areas of your life, and shopping sprees and binge spending are your therapy—until the bills pile into an avalanche that threatens to knock down your sanity and even your marriage. Maybe your financial situation is stellar, but you're praying the Lord will give you a heart of empathy for those in financial hardship. My desire is that this book will do just that. Whatever reason you're reading right now, know this: you, dear reader, are not alone.

Join me as I share my family's story, along with the incredible stories of other families who have beaten financial frustration. I want to give you hope, but I also want to arm you with practical solutions that will take you from financial stress to financial success.

THREE

WHEN YOU CAN BARELY MAKE ENDS MEET

There's never a moment in all our lives, from the day we trusted Christ till the day we see Him, when God is not longing to bless us. At every moment, in every circumstance, God is doing us good. He never stops. It gives Him too much pleasure. God is not waiting to bless us after our troubles end. He is blessing us right now, in and through those troubles. At this exact moment, He is giving us what He thinks is good.

LARRY CRABB, *SHATTERED DREAMS*

When we saw the announcement for a financial planning class in our church bulletin, my heart immediately leapt with hope. We'd been living in the townhouse for over a year, and although we were scrimping and saving money the best we could, we still couldn't make ends meet. *Surely this class will teach us how to rise above this!* I thought. Knowing our financial situation, the staff gave us a scholarship to take the course.

The class was filled with couples of all ages and life seasons, eager to pay off debt, tighten their budgets, and learn how to rein in their spending. But we were in a league all our own. The church met in a school in one of the most affluent suburbs of Charlotte. While other church members lamented how to balance their six-figure budgets, we were barely making it on a fraction of that.

My Bible study mentor's husband was our financially-savvy teacher, and he spoke with a humble wisdom he'd gained both professionally and through life experience. In his sixties and recently retired, Randy Nutter had relinquished a flourishing business career two decades earlier, as the couple opted for more fulfilling albeit lower-paying jobs as professors at a Christian university.

Randy spoke about emergency savings plans, debt reduction, retirement, and even life insurance. He made a case for why Christ followers should prioritize financial stewardship. Financial freedom would allow us to give more, and it would give our loved ones security.

"I always want my wife, Marilyn, to trust me as the provider of our family," he said. "If anything were to happen to me, I want her to know she'd be financially secure because of the steps I've taken to protect her."

We'd enjoyed the first few lessons, but I'd been most excited about one particular class on the nitty-gritty of budgeting. We'd struggled with financial planning since our newlywed days. Back then, we lived on more than twice what we were living on now, but because I'm a saver and Will is a spender, we constantly butted heads on how we should allocate our funds.

A natural optimist, I beamed with excitement as we opened our workbook to the budgeting chapter. I knew almost immediately that Will, ever the realist, wouldn't be enjoying today's lesson. The sample budget was based on a family of four living on $50,000 a year. With what Will was bringing home for *our* family of four, $50,000 a year sounded like a dream. It was frustrating to see that the budget example was so much more than we had. While my heart sank, I figured there must be something we could learn from this class. We were already pinching our pennies, but perhaps there was something else we could try to make our budget work.

But Will knew. He took one look at that budget and shut down. Face red and fists clenched, he slid the workbook to my side of the table and marched out of the room. Flushed with embarrassment, I prayed our classmates hadn't noticed. He stayed in the hallway for the duration of the class. Left alone at our table, I couldn't concentrate on Randy's words. *What was everyone thinking? Did they notice Will's stormy departure? Would Will be angry with me for staying?*

Will wasn't mad at me; he was livid at himself. He was angry that the state of North Carolina didn't pay teachers a living wage—even teachers with years of experience and master's degrees, like him. And he was annoyed that the rest of the class looked at $50,000 a year as a "lower" income while we were making it on less than half that. But "making it" was an exaggeration. We were barely hanging on with the little money he earned each month, and we didn't know how much longer we could survive the emotional stress of living this way.

I approached Marilyn at the end of the class, apologized that Will had left, and explained his disappointment in the course materials.

"I don't know if this is the right class for us," I went on. "We understand the concepts, but the sample budget isn't realistic for us. We're trying to live on much less."

At that moment, Will walked back into the classroom and expressed regret for having left.

"How can we ever get ahead when I'm barely making enough

for us to make ends meet?" Will asked in earnest. "I have all this education, yet I can barely feed my family."

"Would you let us come spend an afternoon with you and go through your finances?" Randy asked. "Perhaps I can see something that you can't see, and we can make a plan together?"

We accepted Randy's generous invitation, and he and Marilyn made plans to visit our home the following Sunday afternoon. They suggested they bring Subway sandwiches for us all to eat—their treat. I thanked God for another meal taken care of that week.

The following Sunday afternoon, after lunch with Randy and Marilyn, Will spread out our financial statements on the kitchen table. No one had seen the contents of our bank account before, but instead of humiliating us, sharing this information with the Nutters started us on a journey of financial freedom. Randy looked over the mortgage statement from our Mississippi home, the townhouse lease, our insurance statements, and our pay stubs. We still didn't own a car, but my parents were letting us borrow their minivan.

The most pressing item was that our tenant had broken his lease five months early and moved out, leaving us with a mortgage payment on top of our rent, which meant we had only $250 a month for food, utilities, and everything else. We had started dipping into our meager savings to pay the mortgage on the home in Mississippi. Once it ran out, we had no idea what we'd do.

After musing over our finances for a few minutes, Randy took off his glasses, rubbed his forehead, and placed our bank statement back on the table. "Well, one thing is clear," he smiled. "You don't have a spending problem."

"We don't?" I was shocked. I was sure we must be doing something wrong to be experiencing so much stress. Wasn't there some area of our budget we could cut to allow for a little breathing room? But here was Randy, a financial expert, telling us we were doing everything right.

"What you have," Randy continued, "is an *income* problem. You simply don't have enough money to live."

We were the working poor.

I don't know why it had never dawned on us before that we didn't have enough funds. We felt financially stressed, but we thought we must be doing something wrong. Surely, we could make our money stretch more than we already were. But we couldn't. Not in the current economy. Not in the United States. We were working, but on paper we were poor.

I'd never heard of the term "working poor" until then, but millions of Americans exist like this. They are working, but they aren't making enough money to pull themselves out of poverty. This results in their debts going unpaid, and in the worst cases, their children going hungry.

According to the Center for Poverty Research at the University of California Davis, "The working poor are people who spend twenty-seven weeks or more in a year 'in the labor force' either working or looking for work but whose incomes fall below the poverty level."[1]

The stigma associated with the poor in America often stems from the false perception that those living in poverty are lazy. After all, the United States is home to the American Dream, with more opportunities than any nation in the world, right? I had, I'm ashamed to say, stereotyped the poor in America this way as well—until I was living as one of the working poor myself. It didn't matter what we did. We couldn't get ahead. And millions of Americans were and are much worse off than we were.

In a 2014 *Salon* article, Karen Weese wrote about the

misconceptions many middle-income Americans hold when it comes to those living in poverty:

> Maybe she wipes your child's face at day care. Maybe he mops the floors at your church. Maybe she makes the beds in the hotel you stay at. Maybe he trims your shrubbery and mows your lawn. Maybe she lifts your elderly aunt in and out of her wheelchair each day at the nursing home . . .
>
> We think of "the poor" as elsewhere, in inner cities or far-off trailer parks, anywhere but here. We tell ourselves that the poor are simply slackers who don't want to work . . . or that the only folks earning wages you can't live on are teenagers working summers at McDonald's, who will of course go to college in the fall.
>
> But it's not true. Fifty-seven percent of the families below the poverty line in the US are working families with jobs that just don't pay enough. These folks are childcare workers, janitors, house cleaners, lawn-service workers, bus drivers, hospital aides, waitresses, nursing home employees, security guards, cafeteria workers, and cashiers—and they're the people who keep the rest of society humming along for everybody else.[2]

As Weese described, the working poor live among us. You may not live in an urban area where homeless men congregate around interstate exits or in a rural village where trailer parks dot the landscape, but suburbia, too, is filled with people just barely making ends meet. It might be the receptionist at your doctor's office, the cashier at your favorite grocery store, your children's classmates, and, yes, even your children's teachers.

Because Will and I grew up in solid middle-income families,

we were unacquainted with financial struggles. The generation before us taught us that if we worked hard and acquired college degrees, we'd be financially secure. But, as our family discovered, anyone can face a financial crisis regardless of upbringing, education, gender, culture, or race.

Our friends Chris and Beth of Ottawa, Ontario, learned the same. Stuck in a career with no room for advancement and excited about pursuing his dream of working in aviation, Chris quit his job in 2009 and moved his family across the country to begin schooling. The family of five lived on a side income while battling the rising cost of living. By the time Chris completed training, the Riccis were crippled with student debt. Another blow came when, just as they were getting back on their feet, Chris experienced a job loss in 2015. In 2016, he finally secured a promising position as the director of an aviation school. The Riccis are infused with hope of paying off their debts and seeing their financial situation improve.

"I used to think people who struggled financially were in another classification," Beth said. "I was somehow separate from that. Now I see that it can happen to anyone—even well-raised, well-educated, smart, and driven people, if the odds are stacked against them for a period of time."

In a June 2012 blog post,[3] Beth wrote, "I have stood in my kitchen crying into my husband's shoulder because my stomach was rumbling, grocery money was depleted until the next payday, and I was so . . . tired of struggling to figure out something appetizing to make from the random things left in my pantry and fridge. I've scrimped and saved and watched sales and planned and packed food for our day trips to the city. I've tried dozens of new recipes for beans and lentils. I've felt guilty for the cheese I give my kids as an easy snack because ten dollars for a block of cheese is very expensive when it gets used up in a week."

DO YOU HAVE A SPENDING PROBLEM
OR AN INCOME PROBLEM?

Perhaps your family is far from being considered "working poor," but maybe you're still struggling financially and can't determine why. My hope is that this book will help you discover the reasons you're financially frustrated and that you'll be empowered to make a plan to give your family breathing room. The first step is figuring out the root cause of your financial challenges.

When we were struggling financially, it wasn't uncommon for me to hear others say they were as well. Once I confided in a friend that the only way our daughter was attending preschool was through a scholarship. She said she wished to apply because her husband only made $50,000 a year, and they had a big house payment. I misjudged this woman as spoiled and materialistic. *If she only knew how little money we're living on*, I thought as we watched our children climb the monkey bars at the park.

I soon learned that financial struggles have different roots, and that's OK. For some, like us, it's a low income. For others, it's poor spending habits. And for many, it's a combination of the two. Or it could be paralyzing debt from student loans, credit cards, or medical bills. Whatever the cause of our financial challenges, we all need grace to get through them.

Randy pointing out our income problem was a turning point for us. We didn't know how to improve our situation until we were staring the real problem in the face. Evaluating your financial position to determine whether you have an income problem or a spending problem can do the same for you.

SIGNS YOU MIGHT HAVE
A SPENDING PROBLEM

The first step in conquering a spending problem is admitting you have one in the first place. How can you acknowledge it if you don't even know you're suffering with this American epidemic? Evaluate your spending choices with the following criteria to determine if you have a spending problem:

You make a budget but never stick to it.

This was an issue for us in the past. We'd create a budget but not a system of checks and balances. If you don't know how much you're spending from day to day, you'll be hard-pressed to stick to your monthly budget. Why put in the work to set a financial plan you don't intend to follow?

You borrow money to pay for things you can't afford.

If you can't afford something, don't buy it—period. If you find yourself borrowing money from parents, siblings, friends, or the bank to satiate your desire for more things, you might have a spending problem.

With that said, I realize there are life circumstances that sometimes necessitate borrowing money for those on a low income. Unexpected medical bills, car repairs, and other urgencies come to mind. The key here is to pay off loans as quickly as possible and work to create enough income (see chapter 13) to allow for emergency funds (see chapter 5) to cover these unforeseen expenses. Proverbs 22:7 says "the borrower is slave to the lender," and borrowing money can compromise relationships.

You shop to satisfy an emotional need instead of out of necessity.

Shopping in and of itself isn't evil, but if you're shopping to fill a void, it's no better than any drug used to mask a deeper issue. Some serial shoppers find they experience a short-term high that's soon replaced by more emptiness—no matter how much they buy.

You max out your credit cards and only pay the minimum each month.

If you're already knee-deep in credit card debt but continue to acquire more and have no intention to pay it off any time soon, your spending habits are out of control.

You make a decent income but continue to overspend on material possessions that fit the lifestyle you want.

Perhaps your family is considered upper middle or high income based on the IRS's calculations, but you continue to overspend in order to keep up with the Joneses or create the façade that you're living on a million dollars a year instead of $200,000. If you're making six figures, you're blessed, but if you spend as if you're making seven, your buying habits will wreak emotional and financial havoc on your household. Keeping up appearances simply isn't worth it.

You hide your spending habits and debt from your spouse.

If you feel the need to hide *anything* you're doing, that's a red flag.

My friend Lauren Greutman, frugal living expert and author

of *The Recovering Spender*, saw her family spiral into $40,000 worth of debt because of her poor spending habits and lack of transparency with her husband, Mark. In a September 2015 blog post, Lauren wrote:

> Most of the debt was unknown to Mark, although I didn't purposefully hide it. He simply never asked, and I never told him. At that point I was managing all of our finances, to help lessen the load on Mark. The problem was—I was the one doing all of the spending and all of the tracking. That was a huge problem because I didn't have any accountability. I would bounce checks often, overdraw *again*, and feel like a terrible wife. I just wanted to be able to help us get out of debt, but I just couldn't seem to make it work.[4]

The good news is that it's never too late to change. Lauren, and many other families like hers, have successfully reined in their spending and gone from financial stress to financial success. Now a national author, speaker, and frequent TV and radio show guest, Lauren teaches others how to recover from poor financial choices.

Your spending may be out of control, but don't despair, friend. There is hope ahead.

SIGNS YOU MIGHT HAVE AN INCOME PROBLEM

Perhaps you don't relate to those with a spending problem. Maybe "frugal" is your middle name, and my story could be yours. Are your financial struggles rooted in an income problem? Do you relate to any of the following?

*You have trouble stretching your budget to cover
basic necessities.*

Do you struggle to pay for groceries, your rent or mortgage, and utilities from month to month? Do you dream about the possibility of one day adding categories like "entertainment" and "clothing" to your budget lines because there's no way you have money for either right now?

You have more month than money.

Do you find you can't afford food or gas during the last week of each pay period and must sit at home and scrounge around your kitchen cabinets for food, even though you haven't purchased any frivolities?

You don't have any debt, yet you're still struggling financially.

Except for our home mortgage, this was our family's situation. We were thankful we had no other debt, but we were still stretched to our limit. When Randy saw that our only debt was our mortgage, it was a dead giveaway that we didn't have a spending problem but a severe income problem.

*When you research poverty level, your family is at
or below it.*

This is the easiest way to determine if your family has an income problem. The cost of living varies for different parts of the United States, so research the poverty level where you live. Find national guidelines at https://aspe.hhs.gov/poverty-guidelines. See your state's Department of Social Services website for more specific standards. You can also discover if your family qualifies for government aid programs, such as Medicaid supplemental insurance, WIC (Women, Infants, and Children), and SNAP (Supplemental Nutrition Assistance Program, which is the same as food stamps). These are determined by family size and income. If your family qualifies for one of these programs, the root of your financial stress could be that you don't have enough money to live.

If you're struggling on a low income, know you're not alone. Millions of families are walking the same path. But there is hope.

For years, popular blogger, author, and speaker Crystal Paine of MoneySavingMom.com and her husband, Jesse, survived on a low income while they committed to remaining debt-free during Jesse's time in law school. Not only did they achieve this goal, but by 2009, the couple was able to save enough money to pay for their first home in cash.

The Paines now give millions of other families hope that they, too, can learn how to increase their incomes, meet financial goals, and stay out of debt. Crystal and Jesse would tell you, however, that their season of living on a low income was not without many discouraging moments. In a January 2012 blog post, Crystal wrote:

> I well remember the days when I felt so desperate. We were barely squeaking by. I was pregnant with our first child. Jesse was in law school and working part-time. I was so sick with my pregnancy that I was unable to continue working and I wanted to stay home with our baby after she was born.
>
> But it all felt so impossible. I was trying so hard to come up with something I could do from home and all my ideas were falling flat on their face.
>
> I was scared and grasping at any straw I could find. I was praying—often *pleading*—and asking God to provide for us.

There were so many moments when I wanted to give in to hopelessness. But, by the grace of God, I kept going, even when everything seemed so dark."[5]

It was during that lean season that Crystal began her business, which has now been a boon for the family. In chapter 13, "Creating More Income," we'll brainstorm ways you can help provide for your family as well.

Whether you have a spending problem or an income problem, know that God loves you and has a plan for your life. How you will overcome this struggle may be part of His refinement of your character, as it has been for me. My prayer is that one day, you'll look back and thank Him for taking you through these challenges and opening your eyes to His provision and purpose along the way.

In the next chapter, we'll look at practical tools to help you curb overspending to get started in the journey out of financial frustration into hope.

FOUR

CURBING SPENDING

*"Why spend money on what is not bread, and your labor on
what does not satisfy? Listen, listen to me, and eat what is good,
and you will delight in the richest of fare."*

ISAIAH 55:2

S he had invited me on playdates before, and I desperately
wanted to accept. I knew his answer already, but I texted
Will at work anyway.

"Hey, Heather asked if I wanted to bring the girls to her
house to play and eat lunch tomorrow. Can I go?"

We still didn't own a vehicle, but we were borrowing and in
the process of purchasing my parents' old minivan, paying them
with every single newspaper check I earned. But we were almost
out of fuel. And Will knew it.

"Can y'all postpone the playdate until next week, after I
get paid?" he texted back. "We just don't have money for gas
until then."

We didn't have much money to spend, and what we did have
we needed to steward wisely. I knew Will was right, but I was
disappointed nonetheless.

CUT SPENDING, NOT QUALITY OF LIFE

Maybe curbing spending isn't hard for you because the money simply isn't there. But maybe you have a middle-to-high income and are reading this book to glean frugal living tips because, no matter how hard you try, you can't make ends meet. On the surface, you look like you have it all together, but you're living paycheck to paycheck and are as frustrated as your low-income friend. Neither of you can make your money stretch.

If you're in the first group, I hope this book will leave you brimming with ideas on how to create more income. If you think excessive spending will never be your obstacle, let me assure you it can happen. When our income increased, it was tempting to spend more because we had felt deprived for so long. Even if you don't have extra income to spend now, this chapter will arm you with resources to keep your spending in check when your situation improves.

If you're in the second group of middle-to-high income earners who are spinning their wheels, take heart. In this chapter, we'll dive into ways you can curb your spending. We'll discuss wise spending habits, talk about ways to stop impulse shopping, and explore wants versus needs. In the next chapter, I'll share realistic budgeting tips, so you can begin living with financial freedom instead of financial frustration. You'll see that curbing spending doesn't have to cut into your quality of life. You can live a happy, fulfilled, God-glorifying existence while spending less money than you ever imagined.

THREE SPENDING MISTAKES
WE WISH WE HADN'T MADE

Will and I didn't use credit cards or go into consumer debt during our newlywed days, but we didn't spend our money wisely either.

The first year we were married, we both taught in public schools, each earning between $30,000 to $35,000. Neither of those salaries made us rich, but our combined income was upwards of $65,000. Still, we pitied ourselves for having a smaller home and less money than many of our friends because we were teachers instead of doctors, lawyers, or corporate professionals.

Four years later we were supporting a family and living on significantly less than what one of us had made that first year. In 2005, $65,000 wasn't bad for a young couple living in the South. We didn't understand how good we had it. And we made big mistakes.

We didn't live on a strict budget.

We had trouble budgeting, and we blamed it on our "lack of income." What we realize now is that the less money you have, the more you're *forced* to stick to a budget (unless you use credit cards, which we'll discuss later in this chapter). We were living on a decent salary in the pre-recession mid-2000s, yet we squandered much of it by eating out frequently, paying for cable television, decorating our home, and even buying an excessive amount of baby stuff during my first pregnancy. If we had decided to eat out one less time per month (or week!), we could have set aside that money for when we started a family.

Although we took a finance class and even met with a financial planner a few times, we never saw eye to eye on what our budget should look like during our first few years of marriage. We spent everything we made instead of living at or below our means. We didn't live extravagantly, but we didn't spend wisely.

We didn't save my salary.

Will and I both wish we had saved my entire salary when it was just the two of us. This could have greatly bolstered our savings account. This is one of our biggest financial regrets.

We didn't wait to buy a home.

We purchased a small starter home in 2006. We had no idea the market would crash just two years later, but we also should have thought through the financial implications of buying versus renting a home (more on that in chapter 14). In retrospect, we should have rented longer and saved for a larger down payment, which would have prevented us from eventually being stuck with an underwater mortgage and a home we couldn't sell during one of the worst economic crises of our nation's history.

The pressure to buy a home is a struggle for many young couples. Our parents' generation believed that renting is pouring money down the drain, but our experience taught us that unless you're ready for the multiple expenses of home ownership, it's better to wait.

You never know when you might face a financial disaster. Wise choices during times of plenty can pave the way for more security when challenges arise.

WHY WE BECOME SPENDERS

Although we've learned to meet halfway when it comes to our finances, Will is a spender, and I am a saver. When we first got married, I was frustrated with how Will spent money. I wanted to save every penny, and he wanted to have a little more fun. To this day, our differences in this area can be a struggle for us, but saving and spending don't have to be all or nothing. Those who enjoy spending can still learn to wisely steward their finances.

Nature or nurture?

For years I assumed that a person's upbringing determined whether he was a spender or a saver, but I recently learned that

...he psychologists believe people are born with a chemical function in the brains that predisposes them to either spending or saving. So while nurture might play a role, it doesn't mean that nature has no impact.

"There are spenders and savers in the same families, kids who grew up in poverty and still develop great wealth, and heirs who blow the family fortune," wrote author Suzanne Kearns in a MoneyCrashers.com article titled "The Psychology of Money— How Saving and Spending Habits are Programmed in Your Brain."[1] A 2007 study published in the *Journal of Consumer Research* showed the different brain reactions individuals display when choosing to spend or save.[2] Researchers noted that insula, an area of the brain which becomes active when someone experiences something disagreeable, is more active in the brains of those who chose to save versus in those who choose to spend. Instead of looking at this as an excuse, those prone to overspending can learn to curb excess buying.[3] We'll discuss ways to redirect yourselves in this area later in this chapter, under the heading "How to Stop Impulse Spending."

A spending disorder?

In extreme cases of excessive spending, the consumer may be suffering from a legitimate psychological disorder. A symptom of bipolar disease, for example, can be irrational and impulsive spending.[4] Some psychologists also believe in a less extreme albeit equally detrimental illness called Compulsive Shopping Disorder.

"While shopping, compulsive shoppers may report feeling intensely excited, happy, and powerful," a 2006 study reported.[5] "These emotions are frequently followed by distress or guilt. They may return purchases or hide them in closets or attics, never to be used."

Compulsive shopping isn't limited to those with money, the

study reported, as "Low-income persons who shop compulsively may do so at consignment shops or garage sales." These shoppers may also suffer from other psychological illnesses, such as mood, anxiety, or eating disorders. Anyone who believes their spending habits might have deeper psychological roots should see a counselor for an evaluation. These professionals can provide coping tools for those with compulsive spending issues.

Seeking to fill a void?

Even if we are predisposed to excessive spending via nature or are nurtured into this habit via our families of origin, I believe these are results of the fact that we live in a fallen, sin-stained world. Every human longs for fulfillment. We seek to find it in different ways. Jeremiah 2:13 says, "My people have committed two sins: They have forsaken me, the spring of living water, and have dug their own cisterns, broken cisterns that cannot hold water."

Instead of seeking God to meet our needs, we have the tendency to fill our lives with things that don't last. For some, these things might be extreme, like sex, drugs, and alcohol. For others, they're more subtle—the thirst for attention, the allure of achievement, the security inherent in money. These are all attempts to fill a space meant only for God. Both excessive spending and extreme frugality can be temporary highs and have the potential to become idols if we don't keep them in check.

Money gives us the illusion of control. We think we can have whatever we want in the moment, not considering the consequences of draining our bank accounts or racking up debt. But those who are classified as "savers" can also be held captive by money's power. Perhaps they don't indulge in high-priced items or use credit, but instead shop clearance racks, sales, and secondhand venues excessively, producing a temporary thrill that soon fades.

In her book *Living Free*,[6] Bible teacher Beth Moore writes, "Many Christians are not satisfied with Jesus . . . We can easily be led into captivity by seeking other answers to needs and desires only God can meet . . . A crucial part of fleshing out our liberation in Christ means allowing Him to fill our empty places . . . God intends for us to find satisfaction in Him—complete, lasting, soul-quenching, emptiness-filling satisfaction."

No matter how much money we spend, only God can satiate the longing in our souls.

HOW TO STOP IMPULSE SPENDING

The good news is that it's possible to curtail unnecessary spending. Having a plan will remove a burden you might not even know you're carrying.

One of my blog readers, an Ohio mom named Diane, learned to curb her spending by planning ahead. "I'm less of an impulse shopper now," she said. "I have to plan everything now and can't just 'fly by the seat of my pants.' I've had to learn how to not stick my head in the sand and hope it all works out."

You don't have to stay stuck in financial frustration forever, and learning how to stop impulse spending will help. The following tips will get you started. Take these tips one step at a time. Before you know it, you'll be well on your way to curbing spending.

Define wants versus needs.

One of the biggest financial faux pas Americans make is defining wants as needs. Our culture is spoiled with excess. We think we *need* a home that provides each child his or her own room. We think we *need* a new vehicle every few years. We think we *need* to outfit our closets with the latest trends and stock our pantries with pricey snack foods. We think our children *need* to be involved in expensive extra-curriculars or they will never grow up to become well-rounded adults. The truth is, we don't *need* any of these. Much of what we see as needs, the rest of the world lives without. In the next chapter, we will use our family's budgeting categories as examples of wants versus needs. If we were living on a low income again, we'd be able to eliminate much of our budget and still survive with basic necessities because we now know the difference between wants and needs.

Give yourself fun money.

There was a time when we had zero margin for fun money, but if you have *any* wiggle room at all, be sure to designate some funds to little splurges each month. It sounds counterintuitive, but setting aside fun money can help keep you from overspending because it gives you a boundary. Even a five-dollar splurge on a fancy coffee once a month can help you avoid unnecessary purchases. Together, we've decided Will should have more fun money than I do. Why? I don't like spending money, but he is admittedly enticed by the latest gadget. A solution is to give him enough fun money to satisfy his spending tendencies without allowing him to go overboard. Right now that equates to Will's fun money being 50 percent more than mine each month, and I'm fine with that—especially since some months I don't spend my fun money at all, so it accumulates! We don't put restrictions on how we spend this money. Will recently spent his on a movie ticket and lunch with a friend. I spent mine on a new cookbook.

Wait before buying.

The true test of knowing if you *really* want something is if you still want it after you leave the store. Delaying purchases by a day, a week, or a month can make a big difference.

Ask yourself, "Do I really need this?"

If it's on sale, but you don't need it, then it's not saving you money to buy it. Would you buy this item—if you had the money—even if it weren't on sale?

Avoid triggers.

Every spender has at least one trigger. Common triggers include grocery shopping while hungry or shopping while stressed or fatigued. Or, it might be one particular store.

For my friend Lauren Greutman, it's Target. "On my journey to recovery, my husband and I decided that I cannot go into Target without another adult, and only with a budgeted shopping list," *The Recovering Spender* author wrote, "To set yourself up for long-term success, honestly identify your weaknesses and make boundaries to keep yourself from hopping over that budget fence you just set up."[7]

I found that even after we had furnished our home, I continued browsing Craigslist on a daily basis. When I realized I was purchasing more than we needed, I had to stop looking at the site. I also removed myself from Facebook buy/sell/trade groups because they only tempted me to purchase things we didn't need. Now, I only rejoin these groups or visit other secondhand shopping sites if I'm looking for something specific.

Stay home.

Perhaps the easiest way to curb spending is to simply refrain from shopping. Shopping is a hobby for some, but spending money you don't have shouldn't be a pastime. I now stick to the very few stores where I get our groceries and household supplies and purchase the rest online. But even with online purchases, you must train yourselves not to browse. If you find yourself logging onto your favorite deals site every day, you might have to take extreme measures and block that particular website from your browser (at least temporarily). Make a goal to only visit online stores when you actually *need* to buy something and not when you're bored and just killing time. While it can be helpful to receive sales alerts via email newsletters, if they make you tempted to buy items you don't need, unsubscribe from them!

When evaluating a purchase, always round up and not down, and consider extra "hidden" fees as well.

If something costs $1.99, you'll pay more than $2.00, not $1.00. Don't forget to factor in taxes and the cost of shipping if you're shopping online.

Live at or below your means.

If possible, live on less than you make. (If you're at poverty level and haven't figured out how to create more income, this might not be possible—*yet*!) Knowing you're spending less than you have will give you financial peace and eliminate stress.

By the time we purchased our second home, we were making enough money to qualify for a larger mortgage. It didn't matter; we wanted the security of owning a house that we could still comfortably afford even if our income dropped again. We chose (and continue to choose) to live below our means.

Stop using credit cards.

I got my first credit card in college. It seemed like everyone else had one, so I got one too. Even as I used it, I thought to myself, *What's the point?* I had enough money to pay cash, so why did I delay payment by using this piece of plastic? *It's not free,* I reminded myself. *I'll pay for this one day. Why would I want to rack up a bill that will accumulate interest and cost me more for the same items in the end?* I imagined how suffocating it would feel to have a large credit card bill at the end of each month. That cured my curiosity, and I haven't used credit cards since.

Credit cards aren't bad in and of themselves; they can help build credit, and some people use them for cash-back rewards. But for those who aren't disciplined enough to pay off the balance each month, using them can open the door to financial ruin.

Credit cards come with a risk even for those who can pay them off. Blogger Jessica Fisher from LifeAsMom.com had been paying her family's credit card bills each month, but the sudden loss of her husband's job left the family stuck in debt. "You never know what will happen!" she warned.

One of my readers, Erin from California, saw her family lose more than half its income when her husband lost his job. At the time, the family was already struggling with credit card debt, and they had little hope for the future. "We reached the point of homelessness and called my in-laws," she said. "We ended up living with them for twelve years."

Perhaps the greatest key to curbing spending is living on a budget. We will dive into the nitty-gritty of how to build your own in the next chapter.

FIVE

BUILDING YOUR BUDGET

"Ants are creatures of little strength,
yet they store up their food in the summer."

PROVERBS 30:25

APRIL 2010

I jolted from bed in a panic as soon as he woke me: "Erin," he panted. "I think I'm having a heart attack. I need you to call 9–1–1. I feel like an elephant is sitting on my chest."

Dread mixed with a foretaste of grief struck me. Will was not one to overreact when it came to medical problems. I ran to the phone and dialed the numbers.

"My husband," I began when the operator answered. "I think he's having a heart attack. Please send an ambulance as soon as possible. Please. Please. Please come now."

I next called my parents, who headed over and arrived at the same time as the paramedics. I could hear the sirens even before we stumbled down the stairs, and the ambulance's bright lights blinded me as I opened the front door. Will was in the bathroom, bent over, when the EMTs entered the townhouse with a stretcher.

"Daddy, please pray," I asked my father. "Please, daddy. I can't do this alone."

I was eight weeks pregnant with our second daughter. Although our crumbling marriage, cross-country move, and descent into a low income less than a year earlier made it feel like our world was falling apart, I knew I couldn't live without Will. *Oh please, God. Please. Please save him. Please let him live.*

I had never dialed 9–1–1 before, much less rode in an ambulance. I sat in the front, with the driver, while the paramedics tended to Will in the back during our seven-minute ride to the hospital. It was the longest ride of my life.

After a scary night in the ER and a visit to the cardiologist for more tests early the next morning, we learned that Will had an infection in his heart that mimicked the symptoms of a heart attack. I didn't care how much the medical bills cost; I was grateful Will was alive. And although we felt like our marriage was barely surviving at this point, this scare reminded us both of the fragility of life and the power of forgiveness. *I have to forgive Will for how he's hurt me*, I thought. *And he needs to forgive me too. We cannot keep living in tension.*

I nervously opened the envelope with Will's ambulance, ER, and cardiologist bills the day they arrived. Even with the little we were bringing in each month, we had kept our emergency fund untouched. Now, we knew, was the time to use it.

THE BENEFITS OF A BUDGET

Even when we were barely making it, we kept that small emergency fund because we knew we couldn't afford not to have one. At our income level, we could be just one emergency away from financial ruin.

We were reminded of the importance of an emergency fund and a budget in general during our financial planning class at the church a year after Will's heart scare. I'll never forget the day Will walked out of that class because he was frustrated with our inability to budget realistically on such a low income for our family size. But in that crisis moment, the tide began to turn for us.

Once we had a more practical picture of the income our family needed to live, we were able to make a plan to reach our goal. We started by making the bare bones of a budget and tracking our expenses to see where we fell short. This helped us realize how much money we truly needed.

While some people may see a budget as constraining, I look at it as liberating. Budgeting can be the tool that removes the shackles from a spender's self-imposed prison of impulse purchases.

Budgeting has many benefits, but three of my favorites include:

A budget holds up a mirror so you can see where you're spending your money.

Have you ever started the month with a full paycheck and wondered at the end, "Where did the money go?" We lived this way as newlyweds, and it drove me bonkers. It's impossible to know if you're spending too much if you aren't keeping track of what and where you're spending.

A budget helps you meet financial goals.

It's difficult to meet long-term financial goals, like buying a house or a car, when you're living paycheck to paycheck. Having a proper budget in place will help you achieve future financial stability. When you know how much you need to save for a down payment for a house, for example, you can divide that into smaller chunks. Allot the amount you need to save each month to reach your goal by a set time. When you aren't living by a budget, frivolous spending can take the place of fruitful savings.

A budget creates freedom.

Living by a budget gives you total control of your money. If I need a new pair of jeans and know I have $100 in my clothing budget, I feel the freedom to go out and buy a $20 pair of jeans. On the contrary, if I need a new pair of $20 jeans but have no idea if I have money in the budget for them, I feel conflicted and guilty about the purchase. A budget gives you the liberty to save for big financial goals, but it also gives you the freedom to spend the money you've allotted when a need (or even a want!) arises. (And yes, I wear $20 jeans! Refer to chapters 8 and 9 for more on how to score clothes so cheaply.)

READY, SET, BUDGET

Our family operates on a zero-based budget, meaning we designate every bit of our monthly income to an area of our budget, and at the end of the month, the budget equals zero. This doesn't mean we aren't saving any money; rather, we designate a portion of our budget to several different savings accounts each month.

I recommend seeking the counsel of a financial planner to help personalize your budget. Many churches offer finance classes with teachers who are willing to coach participants. Two online resources for locating coaches are crown.org and daveramsey.com.

*Here are some steps to follow when setting up your
first budget:*

Add up your total income for the month.

This should include income from side jobs. If your income
fluctuates, you'll need to tweak your budget each month. Base
your budget on your take-home pay. If you're self-employed, you'll
need to factor taxes into your budget as well. This is where hiring
a CPA (see chapter 13) will come in handy.

Track your spending.

It will be impossible to know how much you need to devote
to each area of your budget without determining your normal
spending habits for those areas.

Try this experiment: track all of your expenses for one month.
Keep track of every penny. Save receipts from all purchases. You
won't be able to set up your budget properly without this step.

There are different methods for tracking, and you'll want to
find the one that works best for you. There's always the option to
keep a handwritten budget, which can be a good choice for visual
or kinesthetic learners like me. Studies prove that the process of
handwriting can help solidify things in your memory.[1] Will and
I began our budget this way.

Or, you might consider using a spreadsheet program such as
Excel or Numbers, which are easily customizable.

Finally, a popular option is budgeting through an online
app. Will keeps track of our budget, and this is the method he
prefers. A budgeting app allows you to track your budget via your
computer or smart phone. We both can easily access our budget
this way, anywhere and anytime. There are a variety of options
on the market today—some free and some that come with a small

fee. Mint, You Need a Budget (Ynab), Mvelopes, and EveryDollar are all well-rated apps. (We personally use Mvelopes.)

> ↑ Check out the downloadable resources on my website for a printable income tracker, a printable spending tracker, and more! Just visit thehumbledhomemaker .com/moreresources and enter the password "more."

Designate where your money goes.

At the end of the month, tally everything you've spent and designate those items to categories. Each family will have different categories in their budgets, but the following are ours:

- AUTO: to save money for replacement vehicles
- ALARM: a monthly fee for our alarm system
- AUTO INSURANCE
- CAR MAINTENANCE: includes oil changes and repairs
- CHRISTMAS: helps us not overspend during the holidays
- PHONE
- ELECTRICITY
- GAS
- HOMEOWNER'S ASSOCIATION FEE
- INTERNET
- SCHOOL TUITION
- LIFE INSURANCE
- MORTGAGE: property taxes and homeowners insurance are included in this amount
- WATER/SEWER

- AUTO FUEL
- CHILDCARE: pays a mother's helper who watches the kids while I'm writing as well as date-night babysitters
- CLOTHING
- ENTERTAINMENT: includes eating out, going to movies, and our Netflix subscription
- GROCERIES: includes paper and cleaning products
- KIDS' EXTRACURRICULAR ACTIVITIES
- HOME MAINTENANCE: includes supplies for yard work, light bulbs, air filters, etc.
- HYGIENE/PERSONAL CARE ITEMS
- KIDS' ALLOWANCE
- FUN MONEY
- MEDICAL/HEALTHCARE: includes insurance premiums, copays for doctor visits, prescriptions, vitamins, and supplements
- MISCELLANEOUS: There will always be items that come up that don't fit into one of the other regular categories. A miscellaneous allotment keeps you from overspending when those needs arise. For example, this month we needed to purchase ballet slippers for our girls since they are new to dance class. We pull from this category when the kids have a school field trip, etc.
- TITHE
- CHARITY: above our tithe; can be given to any ministry, nonprofit, or wherever God inspires us to give
- MISSIONARY SUPPORT: a specific amount that supports a missionary family each month
- GIFTS: for birthdays, teachers, etc.
- SAVINGS

Our budget categories are very specific. Others might prefer a budget with more flexibility. When you're tracking your expenses, there might be some months when you don't spend much for certain categories. For example, our HOA fee is due once a year. But since we know we'll need the money eventually, we designate a small portion of our monthly income to the category all year long, instead of being hit with a larger annual payment. Infrequent expenses like these are easy to forget.

Some categories you might have that we don't include pet food/supplies/care or a car payment. Debt payments are also important to include. Remember, you're tracking every single penny!

In addition to funding the above categories each month, we also have the following savings accounts:

- EMERGENCY FUND: As illustrated in the introduction to this chapter, I cannot overemphasize the importance of this budget category. Randy recommended everyone build up $1,000 or as close to it as you can manage to save, in case of any emergency. This includes medical emergencies, cars breaking down, unplanned home repairs, etc. When we use this fund for any reason, we seek to replenish it immediately.

- LIVING EXPENSES: This is a larger savings account we keep in the event of a bigger emergency, such as job loss. This is to help you stay afloat during a financial crisis. If you hit an economic trial, you'll eliminate all "wants" from your budget, so the amount you need will depend on the cost of your basic necessities, like housing, food, and utilities. Financial experts recommend keeping anywhere from six to eighteen months of living expenses in a savings account. We aren't at the higher end of that

yet, but we aspire to get there! Start out slowly, and add
to this savings account as your income allows.

- VACATION/BIG PURCHASES: If you plan for a yearly
  (or more) vacation, funding this account is necessary.
  We combine this with our "big purchases" savings
  account, which is what we use for replacing furniture, etc.
- INVESTMENTS: Since we're self-employed, we allocate a
  chunk of our income to investments each year.

Add up everything you've spent and subtract it from
your income.

Once you have your budget set, this number should equal zero
when you're using a zero-based budget. Don't beat yourself up if it's
not coming up to that right now, though. There may be areas where
you need to curb spending in order to make your budget work.

Make your categories from this exercise the categories of
your budget.

I'm often asked, "How much income should go to each area
of a budget?" Financial planning expert Dave Ramsey gives
recommendations on what percentages to allot to each area of
your budget in his book *The Total Money Makeover.*[2] He notes
that these numbers will "change dramatically if you have a very
high or very low income." Those with a low income, for instance,
will need to designate a higher percentage of their income to
certain categories than Ramsey's recommendations.

In contrast, Ramsey says those with a higher income should
have their necessities budgeted at an even lower percentage than
his suggestions—if they are spending wisely!

Ramsey's recommendations, based on years of experience in
financial coaching, are as follows:

- CHARITABLE GIFTS: 10–15%
- SAVINGS: 5–10%
- HOUSING: 25–35%
- UTILITIES: 5–10%
- FOOD: 5–15%
- TRANSPORTATION: 10–15%
- CLOTHING: 2–7%
- MEDICAL/HEALTH: 5–10%
- PERSONAL: 5–10%
- RECREATION: 5–10%
- DEBTS: 5–10%

A good measure of whether you're spending wisely is if your budget lines up with the above percentages. But remember: If you have a low income, you'll need to spend more on crucial needs—such as housing, food, and utilities—and you'll likely have little or no monies to designate to wants until you begin to create more funds.

THE REAL SAVING SECRET: STICK TO YOUR BUDGET

Setting up a budget can feel overwhelming; but sticking with it can pose the biggest challenge. Keep yourself in check by doing the following:

Track your budget all month long.

To keep ourselves from overspending, Will and I try to check our Mvelopes app daily. Regular tracking helps you to become disciplined about spending, and checking your accounts each day or every few days can also catch potential fraudulent charges on your account.

Connect with your spouse for regular
budget meetings.

We try to meet and discuss our budget about once a month. Our friends Mitch and Megan have a weekly budget "date." A sitter watches their children while they go to a coffee shop to discuss the week's spending.

PROS AND CONS OF
A CASH-ONLY BUDGET

Some financial experts advocate for a cash-only budget since it can be difficult to keep track of what you're spending when you use debit or credit cards. It's much easier to see when cash is almost gone—and when there's none! Many use a cash envelope system, placing designated funds for each budget category in labeled envelopes.

We've considered using a cash-only budget, but we've opted for a combination of cash and electronic debit instead. The only cash portion of our monthly budget is for groceries. Will pays our bills online, so operating with this dual system works for us.

BUDGETING MISTAKES

As I wrote earlier, although Will and I lived with a comfortable income as newlyweds, we made more budgeting mistakes then than we have the rest of our 12-year marriage. After countless conversations with other young families, I know we aren't alone in our budgeting blunders. Have you struggled with any of the following budgeting mistakes?

Not working together as a team

Especially if one of you is a spender and one is a saver, you must get on the same page with your finances. Often, that means compromise.

Not accounting for miscellaneous items

There will always be miscellaneous items that don't fit into your budgeting categories. If you don't use all of this category's funds each month, let them keep building for when needs hit unexpectedly.

Not saving when you are middle or higher income

Dave Ramsey recommends that middle-and high-income earners save 5 to 10 percent of their take-home pay.[3] The more you save now, the more prepared you'll be when financial frustrations take you by surprise.

Designating wants as needs

Distinguishing between wants and needs is key to curbing spending. Needs are required for survival. We can live without a lot if we exercise self-control.

You might *enjoy* cable television, the latest smart phone, and stainless steel appliances, but they aren't necessary for your survival. Food, water, shelter, basic clothing, and electricity *are*. Start curbing spending by eliminating wants from your budget. This will help you pay off debt and eliminate stress during financially frustrating periods. It doesn't mean you can't add these wants back in when you're in a season of financial freedom. These are areas to cut in the short-term.

WHERE TO CUT BACK

- CABLE TELEVISION (check out Netflix, Hulu, or Sling instead)
- HIGH-SPEED INTERNET
- SMART PHONES
- NEW VEHICLES
- EXTRACURRICULARS
- SCHOOL TUITION
- GYM MEMBERSHIPS

Now let's take our family's budgeting categories and strip them down to wants versus needs:

WANTS

- AUTO
- CHRISTMAS
- ALARM
- SCHOOL TUITION
- ENTERTAINMENT
- KIDS' EXTRACURRICULARS
- KIDS' ALLOWANCE
- FUN MONEY
- CHARITY
- GIFTS
- SAVINGS: I categorized this as a want because when you're living on a very low income you might not have the ability to save. However, if you're living on a middle-to-high income, savings should be a need.

NEEDS

- AUTO INSURANCE
- CAR MAINTENANCE
- PHONE: For emergencies, phones are necessary. However, you can find ways to lower your bill and can live without pricey cell phones and services. Our family has been using Ooma, a voice-over-internet protocol phone, since 2008. At this writing, ooma.com offers the device for a one-time payment of around $100, and the only monthly costs are taxes and fees, which are less than four dollars. Republic Wireless is a popular, affordable cell phone service, and pre-paid mobile phones are another money-saving option.
- ELECTRICITY
- GAS
- MORTGAGE/RENT: Unless you put 20 to 30 percent down on your home, expect that PMI (private mortgage insurance) will also be included in your monthly payment. Your best option is to save a down payment large enough to allow you to avoid it altogether (we did with our second home!).
- HOMEOWNERS/RENTERS INSURANCE: These are a must. Shopping around, choosing a high deductible, and opting to bundle home insurance with auto and life can save you money.
- WATER/SEWER
- AUTO FUEL: Check out the GasBuddy app to find the lowest prices near you! Your grocery store may offer gas savings for every dollar you spend. Warehouse stores frequently offer much lower gas prices as well.

- CLOTHING
- GROCERIES
- HYGIENE SUPPLIES
- HEALTHCARE: If skyrocketing insurance premiums are eating away at your budget, check out health share plans. Samaritan Ministries, Liberty HealthShare, Christian Healthcare Ministries, and Medi-Share are four organizations that offer such plans at affordable rates to qualifying members. At this writing, our family is in the process of transitioning to one of these.
- MISCELLANEOUS
- TITHE

DEPENDS ON CIRCUMSTANCES

- LIFE INSURANCE: This should be a *need* if at all possible. It might even be *more* of a need for those living on a lower income because unexpected funeral expenses can trigger financial ruin.
- INTERNET: If you have a home-based business, this is a need. Otherwise, it's a want.
- HOA FEE: Consider these fees when choosing where to live.
- CHILDCARE: This is necessary for working parents; however, check into government assistance programs to help pay for this if you're living on a low income.
- HOME MAINTENANCE: This is a need if you own your own home, which is another reason why renting is better if you're low income.
- MISSIONARY SUPPORT

If we had debt or were living on a low income again, we'd eliminate the wants. In addition, we'd seek to lower the numbers of certain line items in our budget. For example, clothing is a need, but we don't *need* to purchase it each month. Designating fewer monies to categories like this can help you steward your money wisely, even in seasons of need.

Luke 16:10 says, "Whoever can be trusted with very little can also be trusted with much." This is a Scripture I meditated on during our low-income days, and it's one I pray we will fulfill now.

If you're now convinced that it's time to curb your spending, you might be wondering where to start. You might be inspired to downsize your home to lower your mortgage or sell your vehicle to eliminate that car payment. But you can't exactly do either of these overnight. One thing you can do, though, is slash your grocery budget. Won't that require you to lower the quality of your food? Not necessarily. I'm here to teach you that you can feed your family healthfully—on a budget. We'll dive into some ideas in the next chapter.

SIX

EATING WELL ON A RICE AND BEANS BUDGET

Use it up, wear it out, make it do, or do without.

COMMON SAYING FROM
THE GREAT DEPRESSION ERA

After each visit to the supermarket, she sat in the parking lot, meticulously studying her receipt to make sure the cashier had correctly tallied her bill.

"Mama! Can't we go home yet?" my brother and sister and I whined from the back seat of our copper 1973 Grand Torino. Even with the windows rolled down, sweat formed beads on our faces, and our legs stuck to the hot vinyl seats. "What's taking so long?"

"Mama needs to make sure they charged us right," she said. "We don't want to overpay."

If things didn't compute, she marched back into the store, presented her receipt, and requested the correct change.

But my mom's wise financial stewardship started well before the checkout counter.

Every Sunday afternoon, after cleaning up our usual post-church dinner of slow-cooked roast beef, carrots, potatoes, and green beans, my mother spread out the weekly coupon section of the newspaper, covering the round, oak surface of the kitchen table. I imagine by the end of the day her right index and middle fingers ached from being looped so long through the holes of her sharp, red-handled scissors. She held those scissors for hours each week, poised to clip whatever coupon would cut more from her grocery budget.

She categorized the coupons and stuffed them into a sectioned pocket folder. It went with her everywhere, just in case she ran across an item that matched the coupons inside. For years, this was my mother's Sunday afternoon ritual. Although my family never lacked for anything because my father supported us through his job as a corporate hospital administrator, my parents raised me to be frugal. The daughter of a Southern Baptist preacher and the son of a civil service inspector, my baby boomer parents had both grown up in large families where thrifty choices were key. Although he never finished his college degree, my father worked his way up from warehouse stocker to a corporate director for a multi-hospital system. My mother worked at Sears for the first seven years of their marriage, but she achieved her dream of becoming a full-time stay-at-home mom before I—her firstborn—turned two.

By the time we three kids entered school, my father's income could have afforded our family a name-brand lifestyle, but my parents operated out of the mentality that a penny saved is a penny earned. They didn't allow my father's comfortable income to excuse frivolous spending. Instead, they taught us to shop the clearance racks first, that discount stores like Big Lots were magical places full of hidden treasures, and that hand-me-downs were never to be snubbed.

For my parents, those coupons and discount stores and secondhand items equaled money. It was money to feed us, but more than that, what they saved on food and household items they could put toward bigger goals. My parents desired their children to have a Christian education, and providing us with a quality higher education was particularly important to my father, who couldn't afford to attend college himself.

They achieved this dream. All three of us attended Christian schools from kindergarten through high school, and thanks to our parents, we graduated from college debt-free. It all started with a hardworking father and a coupon-clipping mother who practiced frugality and wise spending in every area of their lives.

SAVING MONEY ON GROCERIES
WITHOUT CLIPPING COUPONS

When the recession hit early in my adulthood, the frugality I learned as a little girl was a lifesaver—especially when it came to eating well on a rice and beans budget. During our low-income period, shopping as economically as possible was a must. But even before we struggled, I operated as a bargain hunter. It wasn't until I was well into my twenties that I realized many Americans don't use a grocery budget or make a shopping list before entering a store.

I believe *anyone* can spend less on food and not compromise their health to do so. By implementing the tips in this chapter, you can eliminate the stress of watching your paycheck dwindle with each visit to the supermarket. If you want to live within your means, pay off debt, or save more for retirement, your children's education, or a big dream that's still unspoken, exploring how you spend money on groceries and household items can be the first step.

It might come as a surprise to some that although I grew up with a coupon-clipping mother, I don't use them myself. Instead, I've found ways to save money that work better for my family's lifestyle.

The following tips are ways I save big without clipping coupons:

Shop the clearance bins.

I map out my grocery trips to shop the clearance shelves first. Many stores have these, and if you can't find yours, don't be afraid to ask the store manager what they do with near-expiration-date dry goods and overripe produce that isn't at its prime but isn't bad either.

During our season of low-income living, I frequented a store with a large clearance section. Every time I shopped, the drill was the same: I pushed my cart toward the clearance section of the produce department, then stopped by the meat cooler, then by the rack full of scratch-and-dent canned goods, and ended by the shelf of toiletries. I pretended this was a game—a treasure hunt of sorts.

Most stores don't want to keep bruised or softening produce because it's unattractive and could attract flies or rodents. However, an ugly piece of produce still contains nutritional value!

While shopping clearance for groceries, keep these tips in mind:

Make a plan.

You need a quick, mental plan of what you'll do with the items before buying them. Over-ripe bananas? They make tasty banana breads and delicious smoothies.

Bruised apples? Perfect for homemade applesauce.

Soft tomatoes? Cook them down into a yummy sauce.

Packs of lunch meat? Chop the slices for salads, fry to serve with breakfast, or freeze and take out as needed for sandwiches. There is no reason why packs of meat can't be frozen and eaten over a number of weeks.

Dented canned goods? The food inside tastes fine. You can use these the same way as those with attractive packaging.

Don't overbuy.

I've made the mistake of overbuying clearance produce. While five pounds of mushrooms for two dollars may sound great at the time, if they all go bad before you can use them, then it's two dollars wasted. Without a plan to use or freeze, my "great buys" are really just buying extra time in my fridge as they rot, only to be tossed later.

Be flexible.

Be willing to change your menu. If you've planned on baking chicken tenders with a green bean casserole that night but spy a big bag of lettuce for 50 percent off, can the casserole and serve grilled chicken salads instead! Move your evening's original menu to the next night.

Know food lifespans.

You can freeze meat, dairy, and most produce. This extends the life of the product far beyond the expiration date. Of course, the sooner you eat these items, the more nutritional value they have—another reason not to let food go to waste!

Budget time to save money.

You'll need time to grab the items on clearance *and* make your mental plan. This won't be a quick grocery trip, especially if your store has a large clearance section.

Bring your calculator.

If you're making every penny count, you must know how much you're spending *before* the cashier tallies your bill. Use the calculator app on your phone, or carry a simple pocket calculator in your purse.

If the total goes above your budget, decide which items you'll keep in your cart and what to place back on the shelves.

Cook from scratch.

Buying pre-made meals is almost always significantly more expensive than purchasing ingredients and cooking from scratch. Don't know how? I didn't either. When I got married in 2005, I had three recipes in my repertoire. There was the spaghetti pizza pie, the chicken pot pie, and the taco pie. These pies were easy to make but all consisted of mostly processed ingredients, like cans of soup and frozen pie crust.

Will tired of all three pies within the first week after our honeymoon! I realized that I needed to learn how to cook, and in order to save money *and* improve our health, I needed to learn how to cook from scratch.

Cooking from scratch doesn't mean you won't ever use a recipe. My family hailed my late great-grandmother as an amazing chef, but she never cooked *without* a recipe. There's no shame in simply following directions.

If you've never cooked from scratch, it might be less overwhelming than you think. Steam a head of broccoli instead of buying the pre-seasoned broccoli bites. Make your own mac and cheese with pasta, shredded cheddar, whole milk, and real butter instead of purchasing boxes that come with a powdered cheese substitute. Use day-old bread to make bread crumbs, and use those to bread chicken yourself instead of choosing frozen nuggets at the store.

If you have trouble following recipes, you might gain confidence by taking a cooking class. Check your local recreation center and community colleges for their offerings. If there aren't any local classes available to you, there are now hundreds of courses online.

> Check out the downloadable resources section of my website for a list of my personal recommendations. Visit thehumbledhomemaker.com/moreresources and enter the password "more."

Stretch meals with zero-waste cooking.

The generation who survived the Great Depression lived out the following expression: "Use it up, wear it out, make it do, or do without." Although this adage can be applied to more than food, remembering it challenges me to cook meals that stretch. Some refer to this as zero-waste cooking. Author, blogger, and mom April Lewis has learned the value of using up and wearing out every item in her kitchen. She's made do, so her family hasn't had to do without.

In her ebook *Zero Waste Cooking*, April tells of the epiphany she had when she realized she could feed her family well with the food scraps she'd previously discarded:[1]

I remembered a snippet from a random cooking show I had watched years earlier. The chef used onion skins for making stock instead of wasting them. I thought, 'Well, why can't I use that concept with all my vegetable trimmings?' So I started using them for broths and stocks. Then I thought, what would be the harm in using these cooked vegetable trimmings to make a puree and then strain it to get some sort of soup from it? Before I knew it, there was another idea and another until zero-waste cooking was part of my normal kitchen process. I was using items you normally put in the compost bin to make delicious, homemade food.

Although zero-waste cooking may be an anomaly to some, those in many developing countries have employed this strategy for centuries. Using up every item is a way of life, and they do it well. While writing this book, I spent the summer with my family in Costa Rica. We visited a few touristy areas, but we mainly embedded ourselves in the culture and lived with a Costa Rican woman in her fifties for part of the trip. Fressy, like many Costa Ricans, revels in creating new dishes *out of leftovers*. She lets nothing go to waste. Rice and beans one day become gallo pinto (a traditional Costa Rican breakfast made of leftover rice, black beans, and sautéed vegetables) the next day. Gallo pinto later becomes empanadas by mashing the rice and beans together and stuffing the mixture into pockets of dough. Those eating the leftovers don't tire of the food and may not even realize they're eating the same food day in and day out.

In addition to utilizing every resource in her kitchen, Fressy impressed me by turning everyday trash into decor. I spotted an old rice cooker and outgrown rubber boots she'd transformed into planters, and she'd created a colorful, flowered mural out of recycled buttons and bottle caps.

The concept of stretching meals with zero-waste cooking might stem from necessity, but why not exercise the "use it up, wear it out, make it do, or do without" philosophy at all times to save both money and resources? One of my favorite examples of a zero-waste meal that stretches is cooking a whole chicken. You can serve a whole roasted chicken as the main dish for a dinner, or you can shred the meat, stretching it into more than one meal. Shredded chicken can become enchilada, quesadilla, taco, burrito, or empanada stuffing or the protein source for soups, casseroles, and sandwiches.

You can stretch pulled pork and roasted or ground beef in similar ways. You can use the bones from cooked meats to make stocks for soups and stews. While convenient, boxed broths can be both pricey and unhealthy. It's easy and affordable to make your own by covering bones with water and simmering all day in a slow cooker.

Avoid the unnecessaries.

Are you up for a challenge? I bet you can eliminate several items from your current grocery list without your family noticing. Some items that come to mind include:

- SPICE MIXES: DIY spice mixes are cheap and easy to make. And when you control the individual spices you add to your mixes, you avoid potentially unhealthy "extra" ingredients, like preservatives. One of my favorite spice mixes to make is taco seasoning. I also make a yummy Italian seasoning mix that can serve as both a meat seasoning and the base for salad dressing.
- BAKING MIXES: Baking mixes are convenient and helpful when you have less time than money. But if you're in a season of financial stress and need an easy way to save, taking store-bought baking mixes out of your grocery cart will serve your family well. If you don't enjoy baking from scratch or the time it takes to do so,

you can make homemade baking mixes in bulk batches. Most of these function like a store-bought mix for just a fraction of the price.

- BEVERAGES: My family primarily drinks water. No, it's not completely free, as we have a water bill, but it's cheaper and healthier than consuming soft drinks or juice. Our children have grown up with water as the norm; our younger children still have no idea Coke exists! If your children are older and accustomed to other beverages, ease into cutting them from your lives. Start with half juice, half water or have an honest conversation with your family about how you want to save money and increase your health by eliminating sugary drinks from your diet.

> I've provided links for several homemade spice and baking mix recipes in the downloadable resources section of my website. Visit thehumbledhomemaker.com/moreresources and enter the password "more."

Go meatless.

When we were struggling financially, I would often cook vegetarian meals for the girls and myself while serving Will—who's a huge carnivore—a small serving of meat. I learned it didn't have to be all or nothing. Even one meatless day per week can save money. I made a *lot* of bean dishes, using many recipes from Katie Kimball's *The Everything Beans Book*. You can find it on Amazon.

In a challenge to her readers to spend less on food, frugal living blogger Tiffany of DontWastetheCrumbs.com pointed out that forgoing meat doesn't equal a negative impact on your health. "It is an excellent source of B vitamins, iron, zinc and magnesium, but you can get the same vitamins and minerals by eating a variety of fruits and vegetables," she wrote. Tiffany estimates that going meatless for just one meal a month can save a family nearly fifty dollars.[2]

Garden and/or eat seasonally.

Learning how to grow your own food can be a worthwhile investment of time and energy, especially if your normal grocery budget doesn't allow for fresh, organic produce. If you live in an apartment or home without a yard, gardening will be challenging but not impossible. The HOA of the townhouse we rented for four years forbade planting a garden on the common grounds. Instead, we "rented" land from my parents. We "paid" them with produce from our garden.

Another option for those who don't have yard space is to join a community garden. These shared plots of land are gaining popularity as more families realize the benefits of fresh, locally-grown produce. If your town doesn't have a garden, why not ask your local government about building one?

Don't overlook small space gardening. From tower gardens that don't require soil to container gardening on an apartment patio to growing fresh herbs on your window sill, a little ingenuity can open up more doors and cultivate more savings than you might imagine.

Shop discount stores.

I'm a huge fan of discount supermarkets, especially ALDI. ALDI is a no-frills establishment with simple displays, few name brands, carts that patrons "rent" for a refundable quarter, and a counter where customers bag their own groceries with sacks from home.

These cutbacks come with significant savings to the shopper. I began frequenting ALDI during my newlywed days more than a decade ago, and it's still where I purchase most of our groceries. I even buy our toilet paper there, and it's not the thin, scratchy kind either!

Some people snub stores like ALDI, preferring higher-end establishments, but in my experience, the quality is the same (or sometimes better). Instead of getting frustrated by the lack of choices, I find it liberating that ALDI mainly carries its own brand. This saves me time by eliminating decision fatigue! Other chains similar in price and style to ALDI include Save-A-Lot and WINCO. Even dollar stores usually include a small food section and are worth exploring.

Two other discount stores that sell some groceries are Big Lots and Ollie's. Both are closeout stores, meaning they buy deeply discounted merchandise from stores going out of business. They pass on that savings to their customers. A drawback to shopping at closeout stores is that you never know what you'll find. Unlike ALDI, which stocks regular items, you're never guaranteed to find the same items twice at Big Lots or Ollie's. If you find something you love, stock up, because you may never see it again!

Discounts at bakery outlet stores are also worth noting. When I was a child, my mother purchased much of our bread, crackers, and other baked goods at a bakery that sold day-old and near-expiration goods that she could freeze or feed to us immediately with no harm done.

Shop for bulk items at warehouse stores (sometimes).

It's often—but not always—cheaper to buy in bulk. We've had a membership at either Sam's or BJ's throughout our marriage. Costco is another warehouse store that my friends praise, although

I've never lived near one. The key to shopping at warehouse stores is to make sure you'll actually use the items you're buying in bulk and that you're indeed saving money. Nearly every store lists the cost per ounce or unit of an item beneath its price. Always look at this and compare what you pay per ounce at a warehouse store and at a mainstream or discount supermarket. If the savings is little to none, the store membership might not be worth it.

Keep a price book.

If you find yourself shopping at more than one store in order to get the best deals, it might be beneficial to keep a price book. I first learned this concept from my friend Anne Simpson, author of the ebook *Your Grocery Budget Toolbox.*[3] A price book is a document that lists the prices for the foods on your grocery list, with the regular price at each store you frequent. This helps you quickly assess which supermarket has the best prices for your items. A price book can be any kind of notebook, spreadsheet, or even a memo on your phone.

Buy online.

I absolutely love shopping online because it saves me both time and money and keeps me from becoming distracted by shiny sale items that can make their way into my cart and sabotage my grocery budget. My favorite places to shop online include vitacost .com, grove.co (which price matches and offers free shipping for those with a VIP membership!), and amazon.com. Grove sells toiletries and cleaning supplies, while Vitacost offers the same plus supplements and pantry goods. You can purchase just about anything imaginable on Amazon. All three of these offer subscriber options for greater savings.

Many brick and mortar stores also offer curbside pickup for

online orders. The benefit of fresher foods and same-day pick-up can make this option a huge win for customers, and like online shopping, it prevents impulse buys.

Two other online venues I love are Azure Standard and Zaycon Fresh. Azure delivers both fresh and shelf stable goods to drop-off locations once a month. Splitting bulk orders with friends ensures the best prices. Zaycon contracts with local farmers across the country to provide bulk chicken, fish, shrimp, beef, and pork. Their prices are almost always lower than what you find in supermarkets, and the meat is much fresher. A downside is that you must purchase in bulk, and Zaycon only visits each area several times per year.

Don't forget that shopping online also saves you gas money!

Visit the downloadable resources section of my website to access an exclusive coupon code to help you save on your first Zaycon order. Go to thehumbledhomemaker .com/moreresources and enter the password "more."

Check out store brands.

When I was in college, my roommates teased me because I bought mostly store brands. I attended a small liberal arts university in an even smaller town, and the only grocery store in the one-stoplight community was an Ingles. The store brand was Laura Lynn, and my roommates teased me by saying, "Laura Lynn is Erin's friend."

Store brands might have a bad reputation, but don't overlook them. Often they taste and work just as well as name brands. Try a blindfolded taste test, and you might be surprised! Some store brands are even made in the same factory as the more costly versions!

A word about coupons:

While I don't personally use many coupons, I realize there is real savings to be found in them. Here are some quick tips from my mother—the coupon queen of our family:

Keep coupons organized by item type or alphabetically in a binder or coupon folder. Place the near-expiration coupons closer to the front, so you see them.

Reserve coupons for double and triple days if your grocer offers these. This maximizes the coupon's value!

Stack manufacturer coupons with store coupons to gain even more savings.

Check the Sunday circulars for coupons, but also check out sites like moneysavingmom.com and southernsavers.com for printable coupons!

Whether you employ just a few of these money-saving tips or give them all a try, you're sure to dramatically reduce your grocery budget in no time.

SEVEN

THE MAGIC OF MEAL PLANNING

If you fail to plan, you are planning to fail!

CREDITED TO BENJAMIN FRANKLIN

My sister and I squealed as we entered the red-roofed building with the big yellow arches. Daddy was taking us to McDonald's, and he'd said we could each get a Happy Meal!

Already tasting the salt on our lips, the smell of the grill triggered visions of juicy hamburgers, crispy fries, and bubbly Cokes.

Would the toy in our Happy Meals be a My Little Pony or maybe He-Man and She-Ra? Maybe Daddy would even let us finish off the meal with vanilla soft-serve drizzled with chocolate syrup.

But our excitement began to wane as he placed the order.

"What would you like to drink?" the cashier stood ready to punch in the beverage choices.

"We're not getting drinks," my dad replied firmly.

"But, sir, they come with drinks."

"I don't care if they do," he stood resolute.

Shannon began tugging on his left arm, while I pulled on his right. "But *Daddy*!" we sang in unison. "Happy Meals come with *drinks*!"

Daddy turned his back to the cashier and gave my sister and me *the look* that shut us up immediately.

"I have cold cans of Coke in the car!" he whispered through gritted teeth. "What did you think that cooler was for?"

My sister and I smiled about not having to miss out on our Cokes, but just rolled our eyes at each other when Daddy turned to hand the cashier his money. At just five and seven, even we knew that McDonald's doesn't charge extra for Happy Meal drinks. But our dad wasn't aware of that at the time. As far as he was concerned, he was pinching pennies.

What my dad realized then and I know now is that the real danger to many food budgets is eating out. Even one outing per week at a no-frills eatery can cost our family of six 40–50 dollars, and that's when we order water instead of soft drinks, have our girls split meals, and feed the baby from our plates! This alone can add up to $200 per month to our food budget. By making eating at home your norm and saving eating out for special occasions, you can stretch your income further and meet greater financial goals.

We haven't been perfect in this area. In fact, eating out too frequently became a real struggle for us once our income increased, especially during busy seasons (like while I was writing this book!). What wasn't a challenge at all when we didn't have the money to spend became one of our biggest budgeting downfalls once our income increased. Thankfully, we've learned to rein in excessive eating out with the following simple strategies.

MAKE MEAL PLANNING A PRIORITY

Meal planning helps eliminate last-minute restaurant runs when you realize you have a kitchen full of ingredients but don't have time to cook.

I'm naturally more of a spontaneous person than an organized planner. By my mid-thirties, I realized this part of my personality was causing me *and* my family stress and unneeded spending. Taking the time to develop menus may *sound* inconvenient, but it allows for more harmony in the home. The time it takes to plan ahead is well worth it!

Even a quick mental plan for each day's menu will be better than not having a plan at all. Jotting that plan down first thing in the morning based on what you already have on hand will help you stay on track all day long. It doesn't have to be a complicated system if you're an easy-going person who feels squelched by more intense planning methods. A simple whiteboard or magnetic memo pad on your fridge can do the trick.

THREE BENEFITS OF DINING IN

When you attempt to make a habit of eating at home, it's important to focus on your "why." Why *do* you want to eat at home? Why do you want to make an effort to develop the habit of meal planning?

For me, it's threefold:

Meal planning is better for the health of my family.

When you eat out, you cannot control ingredients, but when you eat at home, you're in charge of what goes into your food and ultimately your body, especially if you're cooking from scratch. Even when we couldn't afford the *best* ingredients, I knew eating at home was *better* for my family.

Although I opened this chapter with a childhood memory of McDonald's, our family now avoids fast food. Excessive sodium and sugars, unnatural oils, preservatives, and food colorings are just a few additives that you're exposed to when you eat out.

Meal planning eliminates last-minute stress.

If you know what meals you're cooking ahead of time, it takes the stress out of the five o'clock scramble. Before I got a handle on meal planning, I often texted Will at 5:00 p.m., when he was just leaving work, and asked him to pick up something for us to eat on his way home.

The sad reality is that this was during a season when we had plenty of food in the house, but I hadn't planned our meals, which meant I hadn't completed the prep necessary to make dinner happen at home.

Whether you plan your meals monthly, weekly, or even each morning (based on the contents of your pantry and fridge), having a menu will eliminate unnecessary stress from your life.

Meal planning saves your budget.

Even if you have your grocery budget down to an art form, if you don't make a plan to cook meals from the food you buy, you'll end up wasting it and spend a small fortune eating out. You can realistically feed your family at home for a fraction of the cost of eating out. The less money you spend at restaurants, the more you'll save for pursuits that embody a greater priority in your life.

MEAL PLANNING METHODS

There are many methods of meal planning, although no set way will work for everyone. It's important to know your personality and give yourself grace to experiment with different ways of planning before you settle on one. The following suggestions can get you started.

Seasonal meal planning

This method incorporates in-season foods into your menu. These are often more affordable since the cost of locally produced food doesn't include transportation. To make this type of meal planning work, list out produce that is readily available and affordable in each season, and plan your meals based on that. For example, you might add more soups with winter squashes and greens during the colder months but more salads with fresh peppers, tomatoes, and cucumbers during spring and summer. You can determine what foods are in season by checking at the SNAP-Ed Connection seasonal produce guide at https://snaped .fns.usda.gov/seasonal-produce-guide or get more specifics for seasonal produce by state at http://www.fieldtoplate.com/guide/

Dish-type meal planning

This method assigns a different dish type to each night of the week. A sample basic menu rotation could look something like this:

- MONDAY: slow-cooker
- TUESDAY: skillet
- WEDNESDAY: casserole
- THURSDAY: baked meats
- FRIDAY: pizza
- SATURDAY: salad
- SUNDAY: leftovers

To make it work, list your favorite meals for each dish-type. When you meal plan, plug in a dish that represents that night of the week.

Protein-type meal planning

This method designates different protein sources for each night of the week. Like dish-type planning, this simplifies the decision-making process and removes the guesswork that can make planning take much longer than needed.

A sample basic menu rotation could look something like this:

- MONDAY: chicken
- TUESDAY: beef
- WEDNESDAY: pork
- THURSDAY: fish
- FRIDAY: vegetarian/beans
- SATURDAY: turkey
- SUNDAY: leftovers

To make it work, list your favorite meals for each protein type. When you plan, plug in a meal that features that protein for its night of the week.

Family meal planning

My mentor Holly, whose children are now all grown, raves about family meal planning, which focuses on the family working as a team to plan meals together. This can either happen in one family brainstorming meeting every week, or you can rotate this chore through each child in your family. Not only does this take a load off you, but it also teaches your children responsibility. By the time they have families of their own, they'll be prepared to plan meals because they'll have this habit. Children can also help with grocery shopping and cooking!

Backward meal planning

I personally prefer what my friend Mindy describes as "backward meal planning." This is my favorite method because it fits my frugal nature *and* my personality. I get bored easily with standard meal rotations, so while planning by season, dish, or protein might be a sanity-saver during busy periods, backward meal planning helps me keep things fresh. Planning this way focuses on grocery shopping first and only buying foods that are on sale or a very good price.

Instead of making a set plan before shopping, I purchase food that's the best deal at the time and plan based on what I have on hand. Recipe.com is a free online tool that helps you find new recipes using the ingredients that are already in your kitchen.

It can take a little innovation to look at ingredients and decide what to cook, but it can save you money in the long run if you're a smart shopper.

The key is to keep meals simple and not diverge into exotic ingredients, which can be expensive. Backward meal planning was a lifesaver for me when we were living on a low income and needed to focus on making our budget stretch with WIC supplemental foods.

DO YOU DESPISE MEAL PLANNING OR SIMPLY NOT HAVE THE TIME?

If you dread the thought of making a meal plan and eating at home, perhaps you're lacking inspiration. One way to cure this? Choose a cookbook and begin cooking your way through it! After struggling in a menu rut a few years ago, I had a lightbulb moment when I realized I had gotten tired of cooking the same meals. Drawing creativity from a new cookbook not only excited me but also helped my family to look forward to meal times more because they'd been bored as well!

I was trying to lose baby weight via the Trim Healthy Mama eating plan, so I requested the cookbook for my birthday. I knew it came with a variety of recipes I could use even if I wasn't following the diet. The *Trim Healthy Mama Cookbook* allowed me to introduce new slow-cooker meals, skillet dishes, casseroles, baked meats, sides, salads, soups, and even breakfasts, lunches, snacks, and desserts to my family. There are over 350 recipes in the book—enough for me to try something new every day for nearly a year! It made me look forward to meal planning and cooking again.

In addition to traditional cookbooks, there's Pinterest, which puts a wealth of recipes at our fingertips. Previous generations were limited to the contents of their cookbooks or to swapping recipes with friends. Today we have no excuse for mealtime boredom. For more inspiration, check out my food boards on Pinterest (https://www.pinterest.com/humbledhomemakr/) or visit the food section on my blog at http://thehumbledhomemaker .com/category/food.

Pre-made meal plans

Even with the suggestions above, perhaps the thought of meal planning sends shivers up your spine. Thankfully, there are people so passionate about planning that they've chosen to do it for you!

Many bloggers post their meal plans each week, either for free or for a small fee. There are hundreds of meal planning services available online. Some post shopping lists, menus, and recipes, while others provide features that allow you to add your own recipes and drag and drop plans into calendars.

While it might sound counterintuitive to purchase meal plans in order to save money, if you struggle with planning, it can help you avoid wasting ingredients and also keep you from eating out. Eat at Home Cooks, Build A Menu, Plan to Eat, and Real Plans are four services I recommend. If fifteen dollars or less for a month of planned meals saves you fifty dollars in take-out orders, then it's worth it.

Meal subscription boxes

If you're not struggling financially at the moment but want to save yourself from expensive restaurant outings, a meal subscription box might be another option. Blue Apron, Plated, and Hello Fresh are three services that have risen in popularity in recent years because they send pre-measured ingredients and easy-to-follow, healthy recipes straight to your doorstep. We've tried Blue Apron on several occasions, and while it's still more expensive than shopping at the supermarket, these boxes are a convenient way to help curb excessive eating out *and* food waste because they only send the ingredients you need.

Now that you have the tools and resources for cutting your grocery budget through smart spending and planning, we're going to consider what is potentially the biggest budgeting downfall for many women: clothing, furniture, and home decor. In the next chapter, we'll explore how you can save money through secondhand shopping. And in chapter 9 we'll explore "shopping" from your own closet. That's right—you might already have what you're looking for.

EIGHT

FROM CLOTHING TO COUCHES:

Secondhand Shopping at Its Best

"And why do you worry about clothes? See how the flowers of the field grow. They do not labor or spin. Yet I tell you that not even Solomon in all his splendor was dressed like one of these."

MATTHEW 6:28-29

When we moved to North Carolina from Canada, we continued a new habit we had picked up from our northern neighbors: recycling. At the time our city didn't offer curbside pickup, so once a week I sorted through all of our recyclables and headed to the town dump. On one visit, I walked away with more than the satisfaction of having completed my environmental duty.

At first, it seemed like any other trip to the dump. I held my breath to minimize the stench of rotting garbage and swatted at flies as I carted my plastic bin filled with tin cans and glass bottles from one area of the sanitation center to the other. Then I saw it: the playhouse of my daughters' dreams.

Why would someone be throwing away such a great

playhouse? I blinked and rubbed my eyes. *Could this be real?* I'd seen this playhouse before at a local park. It retailed for around $500. It had windows with shutters, a sunroof, a fold-out table, and even a sink and cabinet. I knew my two-year-old would love it, and before long, her five-month-old sister would enjoy it too.

An inward battle ensued. *Should I approach the man who was throwing it away? Was that tacky?* He was there to trash the house. I didn't know why else it would be riding on a trailer attached to the back of his truck. We were at the dump, after all.

I walked up to the man's window: "Is that your playhouse, sir?"

"Yes, it belonged to my daughter," he replied. "She's outgrown it. Just needs a little cleaning up, and the door hinge is loose."

I looked over at my mom's minivan—the one my parents had loaned us until we could afford one ourselves—and wondered how we'd make this work. This man didn't have a clue who I was, so I pushed my pride aside and plunged ahead with the next question.

"My little girls would love that house. Can I have it?"

My stomach flipped, but his smile eased me.

"I'd much rather give it away than toss it," he said. "I couldn't find anyone to take it."

I grinned, but my eyes widened as I glanced over at the van. Seeing there was no way the house would fit, the man did the last thing I expected: he offered to deliver it to our home. I asked if he'd mind going a few extra miles to my parents' house. We had no yard, but they had six acres out in the country.

"I'd be happy to," the man said. "I'm glad someone can use it."

That man's trash was this mama's treasure.

Although I confess I felt a bit nervous on the day I found that playhouse, I was actually raised with this kind of resourcefulness. When I was a young child and we lived in a suburb of Raleigh,

North Carolina, we would often find treasures during family walks. From end tables to exercise equipment to the time I rode home on a Kermit the Frog Big Wheel, I knew from a young age that just because someone has thrown something away doesn't mean it's garbage.

When you see your neighbors throwing away something you could use, it never hurts to ask if you can have it. I'm glad I asked about the playhouse instead of watching the man toss it at the recycling station. That little house is still in my parents' backyard more than seven years later; all ten of their grandchildren have played in it.

⁓

While we were struggling financially, God repeatedly provided for us in creative ways. We saw firsthand how God, who clothes the flowers, cares for us (Matthew 6:28). Although our income hovered around the poverty line for years, we never went without. Sometimes it was through the gifts of others, like the playhouse at the dump. Other times it was through smart shopping strategies my parents equipped me with during my childhood. I learned that cultural norms don't have to dictate our reality. Since I'd grown up in a family that valued well-loved, pre-owned clothing and home goods, I had no qualms about buying this way. Instead of causing us to covet newer things, we found that secondhand shopping saved us thousands of dollars.

Some families have no idea where to start when it comes to shopping used. Now, I'm not going to tell you to go dumpster diving, but there are many ways to provide for your family without spending a fortune! This chapter will not only give you a formula for secondhand shopping, but it will also teach you how to love doing it.

SMART SECONDHAND SHOPPING

Be it furniture, clothing, or household goods, buying used helped us make it during our lean years. But you don't have to be struggling financially to benefit from these smart shopping strategies. Whether you're working to curb excessive spending, pay off debt, or simply make wise financial choices, you can learn how to save big by shopping via non-traditional methods.

Craigslist

Our months in Vancouver taught us much about green living. Why not be resourceful and reduce waste by reusing someone else's old furniture? It would be new to us! Having purchased many baby items on Craigslist in preparation for the birth of our first child, we quickly turned to the popular classifieds website to furnish our rental in North Carolina. Within a couple of weeks, our empty house became a home.

Examples of our Craigslist finds included:

- A large, wooden armoire-style entertainment center with TV for $200
- A kitchen table and four chairs for $150 (Note: We later found the exact same table and chairs at a local Habitat for Humanity thrift store. We put the two tables together to create one bigger table, and my mom and I recovered the well-loved cushions from Habitat to coordinate with our nicer Craigslist chairs.)
- A full-size, barely-used couch with hide-a-bed for $100
- Two four-shelf solid pine bookshelves for $50 total
- A glider rocker for our toddler's room for $40
- A full-sized office desk with drawers for $25

- A high chair for $25
- A nine-shelf wooden bookshelf for our girls' room for $10
- A waist-high cabinet we turned into a changing table and baby armoire for $10
- A swivel office chair for $1
- A bathroom cabinet for free (Yes, free! Be sure to check out the "free" section of Craigslist in your area. You might be surprised at what people give away.)

Friends gave us a bedroom suite, and the rest of what we needed was in storage, including a recliner we'd purchased used from my brother-in-law for around $60. Altogether, we spent around $500 to furnish our entire house. In contrast, one brand-new recliner can easily cost $500 by itself! If you're moving, downsizing, or just wanting to save money on home purchases, you can use Craigslist or another secondhand sales site or store the way our family did, too.

It's been more than eight years since we furnished that town-house, but we're still using much of the furniture we found on Craigslist. In fact, we were married for more than a decade before we finally purchased any brand-new furniture.

Furniture has been our favorite find on Craigslist, but there are literally thousands of other items listed on the site. You can find gardening supplies, home decor, electronics, bicycles, scooters, wagons, motorcycles, vehicles, clothing, and even food on Craigslist!

OfferUp

OfferUp is an extremely popular app similar to Craigslist but more photo-driven. Sellers upload images of items they are selling or donating, and buyers can negotiate prices from there. We used OfferUp for the first time while purchasing a few baby items during my fourth pregnancy (which coincided with writing this book). We had a great experience and found the app to be very user-friendly!

New apps like OfferUp pop up frequently, so keep your eyes peeled. Freecycle is another site to consider; it lets you search for items that people are simply giving away!

Facebook buy/sell/trade groups

Local Facebook buy/sell/trade groups function similarly to Craigslist in that one seller lists his or her used items for yard-sale-like prices. On Craigslist, consumers can browse according to category. Facebook has a search function within groups. So on both platforms, you can type in and track down specific items. Craigslist is worldwide and has sub-sites for various cities. With Facebook, users must search or ask around to find local groups. Group members upload images of what they are selling and communicate with potential buyers in the comment threads. As with Craigslist, buyers usually have negotiating power. We bought a set of bunk beds via a Facebook group for one fourth the price we would've paid for them brand new. I only join these groups when I'm looking for something specific, though, because otherwise I'm tempted to buy things we don't need.

Consignment

When I was expecting our first daughter, I discovered children's consignment shops and sales. One benefit of consignment shopping is that most places have strict quality control, making the inventory much more desirable than what you might find at thrift stores, yard sales, or via Craigslist, OfferUp, or Facebook. However, the items are usually priced higher since a third party is involved.

In addition to physical stores, online consignment businesses now allow consumers to shop secondhand from the convenience of home. Popular sites like Schoola.com, Swap.com, and thredUP .com boast that customers can save anywhere from 50 to 90 percent off retail prices. One disadvantage of these is that they require you to spend money on shipping or spend a minimum amount before getting free shipping. But their advantages, compared to brick-and-mortar stores, are that their inventory is usually much larger and you can customize your search.

Schoola, which specializes in children's clothing but also sells women's items, operates as a cross between an online thrift store and consignment store. Its inventory comes from donations, and those who send in items don't see any profit. Rather, the donors choose schools to receive a portion of the earnings. The inventory from Swap and thredUP comes from consignors sending in items. If the items sell, they will earn a percentage of the profits. ThredUP is the most upscale of the three. They are pickier about what they accept, and the prices are higher. If you have a penchant for top brands, you'll be able to save money with thredUP over buying new at department stores.

Thrift stores

Thrift store shopping is in my family genes. My paternal grandmother began thrifting more than fifty years ago, when my father was a pre-teen. Then, it was her hobby. When she became a single mom with two of her five children still at home in the mid-1970s, she turned this pastime into her livelihood. For the next 25 years— until her death—Granny fully supported herself by buying and reselling high-end items from thrift stores and yard sales.

Having inherited the thrifting knack from his mother, my dad is now a thrift-shopping expert. When he retired a few years ago, he began shopping at our local Goodwill and Habitat for Humanity stores twice a week. While thrift stores have a reputation for being smelly, dirty, and simply undesirable, that isn't true in many cases. My father finds top-brand clothing, shoes, handbags, jewelry, china, and more on his shopping trips. He now uses his smart phone to help him determine their value, but he'll sometimes come home with a buried treasure he had no idea he was snagging.

"One time I bought a pair of black Tony Lama boots that I told your mom I wanted to mow in," he told me. "She said, 'You are *not* mowing in *those* boots!'"

My father didn't realize he'd just paid $15 for a pair of $1,300 boots! It's not uncommon for my dad to spot brands like Nautica, Cole Hahn, Polo, Izod, Eddie Bauer, Brooks Brothers, and Mikasa, just to name a few. He even has a knack for finding new items with the tags still on them!

Yard sales

Whether your region calls them yard, garage, or rummage sales, they're all one and the same. If you're looking for the lowest prices possible, this will be your secondhand shopping method of choice. While they can be hit or miss, it's possible to find some high-valued items. Our four children are still playing with several Fisher Price Little People toys I bought at a yard sale when I was expecting our firstborn a decade ago!

Because most sellers simply want to get rid of things, you can negotiate more at yard sales than at other secondhand shopping venues. But once you negotiate, there's no possibility of returning your purchase, so make sure you buy what you really want or need, apart from the draw of a good deal.

Estate sales

Estate sales are similar to yard sales, with more variety and vintage potential, but keep in mind that negotiating is taboo at estate sales. If you stop by a sale near its end, you're more likely to find items marked down. Showing up early, though, will guarantee you discover the best items before another buyer snaps them up. Often you can find estate sales by keyword searching on Craigslist or in your local newspaper.

SECONDHAND SHOPPING TIPS

While it can be a fun hobby to browse secondhand venues—and it can even turn into income if you buy and resell—if you're struggling with financial anxiety, I recommend you only shop when you truly need something. With that in mind, the following tips should help you get the most bang for your buck when buying used:

Craigslist/Facebook groups/OfferUp

- Make a list of what you need.
- Start checking Craigslist, Facebook groups, and OfferUp daily for the items on your list.
- When you see an item you want, email or call the seller and ask if the price is "firm." If not, don't be afraid to negotiate! Most sellers will name a price with "OBO," which stands for "or best offer."
- Eye before you buy. Don't commit to any purchase before seeing the item. Go quickly, as most sellers don't wait if they get a better offer.

- Take someone with you and/or meet in a public place. Sadly, some people are dishonest, and buyers have gotten themselves into dangerous situations by being too trusting. If you have a bad feeling about the situation, don't go.
- Never pay before you see the item. Some scammers will ask for a "deposit" via electronic transfer or Paypal. This is a telltale sign that the lister is a fraud.
- See another item you like at the seller's home? Ask if it's for sale! We snagged our changing table at the house where we bought a bookshelf because we asked if it was available (and then grabbed a free cabinet from the side of the road in the same seller's subdivision!).
- Make items your own. We stained the pine bookshelves to match the rest of our darker living room furniture, and we painted the bunk beds black to match our black crib.
- With furniture especially, be sure to check for signs of dirt, bugs, etc. Some people refuse to purchase upholstered furniture at all. Forgo buying used mattresses unless you do so from someone you know extremely well.
- Make sure electronics work before you buy. Check for broken hardware and missing pieces on all purchases.
- Realize the risk. It's highly unlikely a secondhand seller will accept returns and issue refunds. Be sure you're 100 percent satisfied and confident in your purchase before buying.

Consignment

- Shop for items that are hard to find at discounted prices, like boutique brands and school uniforms. At one of our local consignment venues, I've been able to find most of my children's school uniforms, already embroidered with the logo, for less than what I would pay for just the embroidery on a new item!

- Look for new items. With online stores like thredUP, you can even filter to search specifically for new pieces with the tags still on them!

- Inspect items thoroughly. Consignment shops typically offer higher-quality items, but it's not uncommon to find small stains or holes. (Note: a downside to online consignment stores is that you will not be able to check over the items before buying them.)

- Ask about return policies. This will help you make wiser purchases.

- Know your children's sizes. Not all shops offer dressing rooms. Don't resort to guesswork when you're purchasing shoes and clothing that you might not be able to return. If you're still unsure, have your child try on a pair of pants, a shirt, and shoes at home and take those with you to the stores as a way to measure whether the clothing will fit. For online purchases, I note the brand of the item I want to buy and find the measurements guidelines on the brand's website. I then measure myself or my children before making the purchase.

- Take a clothing inventory before leaving home. When prices are low, it's easy to overbuy. Before I shop consignment, I take note of what we already own. I then make a list of exactly what we need, so I'm not swayed to buy more than what will fit in our drawers.

Thrift stores and yard sales

- Shop early and often. Inventory is constantly changing at thrift stores, and yard sales are usually one-day events. Professional yard sale shoppers hit the road before 6:00 a.m.

- Negotiate! This is especially true with yard sales, but *some* thrift stores might also be up for bargaining (especially if you're a regular customer!). At yard sales, don't be afraid to ask for half off the asking price. If you're offering to buy multiple items, ask for a flat reduced price for all of them together.
- Shop in affluent areas where you're more likely to find higher-end items.

What if you want to purchase new items? Are there ways to save money without buying used? First, let's explore what you already have in order to see if you even need what you're wanting. But don't worry. I'll also give you tips to buy new without breaking the bank. You'll find both in the next chapter.

NINE

FIRST, SHOP AT HOME; THEN SHOP SALES

A penny saved is a penny earned.

BENJAMIN FRANKLIN

A few years ago, I decided my wardrobe needed a complete overhaul. I've never been a fashionista, but I was keenly aware that I'd been living in a fashion frump after more than six years of back-to-back pregnancies and breastfeeding. The clothing I wore was out of style and ill-fitting. My only problem? I didn't want to spend a lot of money (nor did I have the money to spend!). My friend Holly suggested that her fashionable cousin, Candace, help me shop in my own closet, putting together stylish outfits from pieces I already owned. I was floored at the many beautiful outfits we put together without spending a dime! Candace was tactful but truthful about what items I should ditch, and she gave me savvy tips on what I should (and shouldn't) coordinate.

"Those mom jeans? You'd better never leave the house in those again!" Candace teased. "But this black angled cardigan?

It's going to be your new favorite piece. We can make it work for several outfits, and it will flatter your mama curves."

You might be surprised at how many outfits you have lurking in your closet or in other storage areas. I'm now convinced that everyone can save money by "shopping" from their own belongings.

SHOPPING FOR CLOTHES
IN YOUR OWN CLOSET

Most Americans live with closets that are so packed with clothing, they are surprised to find what they need already hiding among the hangers! I know that was the case for me! The following tips will make for a successful "shopping" experience.

Enlist a friend to help.

This friend *must* be honest, and your most stylish friend is the ideal candidate. If you don't have a friend like this, recruit a friend of a friend. (That's what I did!)

Pull everything *out of your closet.*

Yes, I mean *every single item.* You need to see what's buried in your closet. There might be more than you think! I found that cute cardigan I mentioned before. I had no idea it was in there, and I still don't know how I acquired it, but I'm glad we found it! You'll also want to pull things out of your drawers. Lay everything on your bed, grouping pieces according to category (shirts, pants, etc.).

With your friend's help, put together outfits.

Now comes the fun! Match up pants and shirts, skirts and blouses, etc. Don't forget shoes and jewelry!

Try on the outfits.

This is where you'll put feelings aside. Try on every single outfit, and ask your friend for honest feedback. If an outfit looks cute on the hanger but not so great on you, why keep it?

Unless an outfit makes you feel amazing, donate it!

There's nothing lost in passing on clothing to others who might need them. Less can be more. Fewer clothes that make you feel confident are better than a closetful that make you feel drab. What doesn't work for you might look fabulous on someone else.

Hang the clothes together as complete outfits *in your closet.*

Previously, I hung all like items—shirts, pants, dresses, etc.— together, but it saves time and makes sense to hang complete outfits. I can easily choose which outfits to wear and not waste mental energy trying to decide which shirt goes with which pair of pants. Holly also suggested I print pictures of the outfits to place on the wall of my closet to help me reassemble them when I'm putting away laundry.

Make a list of items needed to finish your wardrobe.

You may find you need a few things to round out your wardrobe. For me, it was skinny jeans and flats. Armed with your shopping list, check out local consignment shops, thrift stores, yard sales, and store clearance racks. By the time you finish this book, you'll know how to get the best bang for your buck, and doing so will be more fun than you ever imagined.

You can also use the "shop from your own closet" method for your children's clothing, and you can encourage your husband to try this technique as well. When it comes to home decor and other household goods, try "shopping" from the other storage areas of your home.

As a bonus, this can double as decluttering! When I first "shopped" from my own closet, I filled the back of my minivan with bags of clothing to donate. The result was a closet that felt lighter, more manageable, and less stressful but was filled with clothing I loved.

There are two more ways to add to your wardrobe (or home in general!) at no cost to you: hand-me-downs and exchanges.

THERE'S NO SHAME IN HAND-ME-DOWNS

When I was a kid, even though my parents could afford new clothing, we wore plenty of hand-me-downs. My parents refused to pay full price for anything, and when a friend, relative, or neighbor offered them a bag of children's outgrown clothing, my mom and dad accepted it with no qualms. Since my parents very rarely bought name-brand items, my sister and I delighted in these hand-me-down bags because oftentimes, they meant we could sport higher-end clothing. If someone offers you free clothing and you need it, there should be no shame in accepting it. Even as a woman in my mid-thirties, I still wear hand-me-down clothing. In fact, a good portion of my wardrobe consists of clothing that my dad's former coworker gave me when his wife passed away. She was a fashionista who wore the best brands on the market. Much of the clothing her husband gave me still had tags on it. I get compliments every time I wear her clothes, and it's a reminder to pray for her family.

Start a clothing exchange.

If you have unwanted clothes in your closet and wish you could make room for more but can't afford a new wardrobe, consider starting a clothing exchange with a group of friends. A church where I attended a weekly Bible study hosted a women's clothing exchange just when I needed it the most because of back-to-back pregnancies and subsequent weight gain at a time when our lack of income prohibited me from buying anything new. Women of all incomes and life seasons participated, and it was more like a fun girls' night than a charity event. At a time when I battled extreme anxiety about the state of our bank account, there was no shame, no stigma. I walked away with a wardrobe that lasted me through those really lean years.

A clothing exchange can be as organized as you want to make it. You can include a small group of friends, or you can open it up to your entire church or a community organization. I have only participated in women's clothing exchanges, but I have heard of exchanges for children's clothing, toys, and gear as well. The beauty of an exchange is that it allows participants to rid their homes of unneeded items while snagging what they *do* need—for free!

Are you intrigued by the idea of a women's clothing exchange? Why not start your own? While developing a program that will help you increase your wardrobe without spending any money, keep these tips in mind:

Find a location.

If your church women's ministry is hosting the event, then the logical location is most likely the church building. Other possible venues could be your workplace, a school gym, a community center, or someone's home.

Determine participation requirements.

Will you require participants to donate clothes in order to receive them? If so, will you require a certain number of donations?

Will you require that participants be church or group members, or will you open the exchange to the public? Must participants serve volunteer hours in order to benefit from the event?

At the exchange where I participated, we were not required to donate clothing, but we were limited in the number of items we could take home. The exchange was only open to ladies of the church or Bible study group. Volunteers ran the event, but we didn't have to volunteer in order to shop.

Organize the clothing and accessories.

At a time when we could barely afford groceries, attending clothing exchanges gave me dignity because they were well-organized and open to women of all incomes. Organizers made sure the donated items were attractively displayed, the way they would be in a store. Clothing was arranged according to size and season, with racks designated for dresses, skirts, blouses, pants, coats, maternity, pajamas, workout clothing, jeans, business suits, etc. There was a separate area for shoes, handbags, jewelry, and accessories.

Provide a dressing room where participants can try on clothes.

Since the clothing is free, there are no returns. There will only be so many clothes to go around, and providing an area where people can try on clothing can ensure that each participant leaves with items she will actually wear.

Determine what to do with leftover items.

Will donors be allowed to reclaim their items, or will you pick a local charity to receive the excess? The church where I participated donated leftover items to a local women's shelter.

Just like shopping from your own closet, you can use the exchange idea for other home items. I think an exchange of home decor, small appliances, or even furniture would be especially fun. What you no longer have use for might be just what your friend is seeking, or vice versa!

BUYING NEW WITHOUT BREAKING THE BANK

So far, we've discussed buying used and acquiring items for free. You might be thinking "Does this woman *ever* buy new?" The answer is a resounding "Yes!" It *is* possible to save big while shopping for new items.

Clearance racks

My parents taught me to head to the back of the store when we shopped. By the time I was a teenager, this had become habit. To this day, I rarely glance at the full-price items in the front of a store, especially when I'm shopping for clothing. Instead, I start at the clearance racks.

Most stores offer at least a small clearance section year-round. The best time to shop clearance clothing, though, is at the end of each season. At stores like Kohl's and Target, I've found clothing for my children up to 90 percent off retail! The key here is to shop one season ahead. I shop for fall and winter clothing at the beginning of spring and for spring and summer clothing at the start of winter. Stores need to move inventory to make room for new items, so they're willing to sell at extremely low prices. In fact, shopping clearance is often more affordable than consignment because the store is more invested in moving inventory than in turning a profit. Some families have created side businesses by buying clothes on clearance and reselling them on eBay, consignment, or Craigslist!

In addition to clearance racks, most stores offer clearance sections online. A downside is that you may have to pay for shipping. However, many online stores provide free shipping if you spend a certain amount. Shopping clearance is the ideal time to use coupons, gift cards, and other discounts. It's even possible to acquire items for free sometimes!

In a similar vein, check out local scratch and dent stores for home appliances. And don't shy away from asking retailers at mainstream stores what they do with display items. They will often sell these at clearance prices as well!

Outlet stores

It might come as a surprise that my penny-pinching parents enjoy shopping as a hobby. They get a thrill over how much they save, rather than how much they spend. When I was a little girl, my parents shopped at every outlet mall they could during road trips. They'd purchase an entire year's worth of clothing for us kids for a fraction of what they would have spent at retail prices.

In the 1980s and 1990s, most outlet stores carried overstock or slightly imperfect inventory, which is what made the items so cheap. That isn't always the case today. While prices are still often better than what you find at retail stores, even at outlets you should head to the clearance sections first to save even more money.

Loyalty rewards

Many stores offer loyalty benefits for frequent shoppers. At Kohl's, for example, customers can earn free credit that can be applied toward future purchases. This is an easy way to score deeper discounts or even free items. But these discount programs should come with a caveat. Because customers earn more the more they spend, this can encourage unnecessary spending. If you already struggle with a spending problem, loyalty cards might not work in your favor. If you have to pay for a rewards card, be sure you use it enough to cover the cost. Pick just one or two venues to be your loyalty program stores for optimal saving.

Closeout stores

As I mentioned in chapter 6, "Eating Well on a Rice and Beans Budget," closeout stores like Big Lots and Ollie's are great places to pick up items at shockingly low prices. While you can find food at many of these stores, you can also find a plethora of other household goods, from furniture to school supplies to tools and gardening equipment to cleaning supplies to home decor to gifts to clothes and much more! These stores are hit-or-miss, but you are almost always guaranteed to discover some hidden treasure when you shop these venues. Our new TV stand was a Big Lots find. We get compliments on that TV stand when we have guests in our home, and I have no problem telling people it came from a closeout store.

Shop around

When buying new or high-priced items like furniture, it pays to shop around. While there are merits in customer loyalty, especially for local businesses, if you are in a season of financial frustration, you need to be willing to shop at more than one location. You might be surprised to find that different stores will offer the same item at different prices.

Online discounts

The sky is the limit when it comes to how much money you can save by shopping online. Our parents didn't have this luxury, but I'm thankful for the time and money it saves me! There are new money-saving apps and websites constantly popping up that can help track down coupon codes, discover stores with the best prices, and even reimburse you just for shopping at certain locations. Since these apps and sites seem to come and go, I'll focus on those with a long-standing reputation. But to get real-time reviews on money-saving apps, be sure to sign up for my newsletter at thehumblehomemaker.com, or check out my favorite money-management site for moms, moneysavingmom.com.

Some popular money-saving websites include:

- EBAY.COM: eBay is a popular buying and selling website that has been around for years. You can find anything and everything on eBay. One warning, however: some sellers overprice items on eBay. Just because it's on eBay doesn't mean it's a good deal.
- SWAGBUCKS.COM: Swagbucks is a popular app that allows people to earn money to spend at a variety of stores simply by using the Swagbucks search engine and taking online surveys.
- EBATES.COM: My mom is a huge eBates advocate. This site will give you rebates if you use eBates.com to purchase items from popular stores across the web.

Whether you purchase your family's clothing and other home goods used or new or find them in your own storage spaces, can you see God's provision in your lives? Looking at our possessions from this angle can give us a new perspective and help us praise God in times of plenty *and* in times of want. We'll examine how to recognize God's provision for all of our needs in the next chapter.

TEN

PERSIMMONS AND PROVISION

*The Israelites said to them, "If only we had died by the L*ORD*'s hand in Egypt! There we sat around pots of meat and ate all the food we wanted, but you have brought us out into this desert to starve this entire assembly to death."*

Then the Lord said to Moses, 'I will rain down bread from heaven for you. The people are to go out each day and gather enough for that day"

. . . . Everyone had gathered just as much as they needed.

EXODUS 16:3–4, 18

WINTER 2011

I'd never heard of persimmons. The classified advertisement said they were fruit, and it said they were *free*; that's all I needed to know. So I answered it. I emailed the anonymous poster and said I would take her up on her offer of free persimmons. When I googled the address, I saw that it was near the lake, in an affluent neighborhood.

I bundled up the girls, strapped them into their car seats, and headed across town. The house was large but not as extravagant as I'd imagined. I parked in the driveway and walked up the brick steps to the front door. Before I could knock, two women—one middle-aged and one elderly—opened it.

"You must be the lady coming for the persimmons," the younger woman said, smiling.

"Oh, yes," I answered. "They'll be such a blessing to my family."

She reached out to shake my hand, introduced herself, and explained that this was her mother's house. The older woman's trees were full of persimmons, and she couldn't use all the delicious fruit.

"Can you tell me what, exactly, you do with them?" I blushed. I didn't want the women to know I'd never even seen a persimmon, much less cooked with one.

"Oh, all kinds of things!" the younger woman said, laughing. "You can eat them whole, but we love to bake cookies, muffins, and cakes with them. You can also puree them and use them the same as you would applesauce in a recipe."

The ladies let me take my pick of the fruit, and I filled the box they set out for me. They then offered me several slices of freshly-baked persimmon pound cake. It smelled scrumptious, so I accepted the gift. After all, it was snack time. The girls would be hungry and more than happy to eat a piece of cake.

Those women never knew how that box full of persimmons would go on to provide breakfast for our little family during a season of financial hardship.

LIKE MANNA IN THE WILDERNESS

God is the Great Provider. I'd known that since childhood, but I didn't truly recognize His personal provision for our every need until I was in my early thirties, with two young children and another one on the way, a husband who worked several extra jobs on the side, and an income that still didn't cover all our expenses.

It was a desert season. We were frustrated by trying to make our money stretch, I was depressed, and our marriage was stuck in neutral. The tunnel looked dark, and I couldn't see a way out.

On paper we were poor, yet I can look back now and see how I richly experienced God's presence during that time. With a burgeoning belly, one toddler on my hip, and another wrapped around my knees, it wasn't uncommon for me to open my near-empty refrigerator and whisper prayers of petition wrapped in thanksgiving: *God, you will meet our every need. You have never failed us. You are in control.* It was a "this is it" season. *This*, I would tell myself, *is when our faith is proven real.*

It wasn't the first period in my life when I'd been forced to depend on God alone. A key example is the day my friend Courtney died tragically in a car wreck. I'd known Jesus as my personal Savior for ten years at that point, but at just nineteen, my faith was still mostly untested and immature. I felt empty, alone, and abandoned by God. The day I lost Courtney is still clear in my memory. Stifling tear-filled screams as I clenched and unclenched my fists, I crumpled to my dorm room floor and clasped my hands over my heart. "Where are you, Jesus?" I asked audibly, as I nearly hyperventilated. "Where *are* you now? Why can't I *feel* you? Are you even *real*?"

Through heavy-hearted days during which sleep evaded me, God slowly, gently began to heal my grief. He soothed me through 1 Peter 1:6–9:

> In all this you greatly rejoice, though now for a little while you may have had to suffer grief in all kinds of trials. These have come so that the proven genuineness of your faith—of

greater worth than gold, which perishes even though refined by fire—may result in praise, glory and honor when Jesus Christ is revealed. Though you have not seen him, you love him; and even though you do not see him now, you believe in him and are filled with an inexpressible and glorious joy, for you are receiving the end result of your faith, the salvation of your souls.

Fast forward more than a decade, and the circumstances of this season were certainly different from that heartbreaking day in 1999. But in this trial, too, God was building our faith. Just as I personally had learned to trust Him as I walked through a season of grief, our family would learn to trust God during a season of need. It had been easy to trust Him when we weren't in want. Now that we were, God was cultivating in us a deeper faith, a stronger trust in His provision.

I started looking at and crediting each and every incident— from the government WIC checks to the box of persimmons—as God's provision for our family. Like manna in the wilderness, the Lord provided again and again and again. As time passed, I saw it more clearly than ever, and looking back, I realize He provided all along.

The manna or "bread" from heaven in Exodus 16 wasn't what the Israelites *wanted*, but it was what they *needed*. It wasn't extravagant, and in their shortsightedness, forgetting the turmoil the Egyptians inflicted upon them, they grumbled against God's provision. Still, it met their needs.

Born in the United States to a semi-affluent family, I'd never experienced true want. I'd lived in abundance, as most of us in this country do. But now that my family was in need, God proved that we truly lacked nothing. Perhaps we desired more, but just as the Lord had provided for the Israelites in the desert, He covered our *needs*.

DIFFERENT FORMS OF PROVISION

Whether it was through a playhouse at a garbage dump or fruit from a stranger, God has consistently provided for our family's needs. The ways He can do this for *you* too are unlimited. I've put together a list of potential opportunities for provision here. My hope is that by the end of this chapter, you'll see how clearly God has provided for you, in both the unexpected and in the ordinary.

Good deals, great finds, and unexpected gifts

Have you ever opened your mailbox to find a higher tax return than you anticipated, a rebate from an item you purchased, or an unexpected check? None of these are random, my friend. When we cultivate a spirit of gratitude for God's provision, we'll see clearly how He cares for us in tangible ways. (And I argue that He gives to us so we can, in turn, give back to others as well.)

When our firstborn was three, her pediatrician diagnosed her with gluten intolerance. At the time, we were struggling to buy basic groceries. How would we rise to the overwhelming challenge of fitting expensive gluten-free foods into our budget? Not long after her diagnosis, I was poring over my weekly meal plan when I heard a knock on our front door. It was one of Will's coworkers, Kathy. Kathy has celiac disease, which had forced her to go gluten-free several years earlier. She knew how expensive gluten-free foods cost, and she knew how little money we had. She took it upon herself to purchase some extra gluten-free groceries that day. Among them were gluten-free animal crackers for our little girl.

I held back tears as we accepted this surprise gift. It was enough food for the next few days, and it helped me realize we could trust the Lord to meet our future needs because He showed over and over that He met our present ones.

Another time, my college roommate's parents offered our little family an entire week at their beach house. Our marriage was stuck in survival mode, I was expecting our second daughter, and we hadn't had a real vacation in years. The tiny town of Edisto, South Carolina, provided a much-needed respite during that week. We thanked my friend's parents for their generosity and told them how they were testaments to us of God's provision, not only for our physical needs but also for our hearts during a turbulent time in our lives.

I believe that God provides for *all* of our needs; nothing is coincidental. The wild blackberries we foraged from my parents' back yard? Those were from God. The packages of organic rolled oats that showed up at Big Lots? They were from God. The gluten-free cake mix that landed on the clearance shelf for a fraction of the retail price? Yes, from God as well.

When we choose to believe events like these are simply coincidences or somehow our own doing, we fail to credit the One who has orchestrated our entire lives (Psalm 139:16), the One who has promised to provide for all our needs (Philippians 4:19), the One who deserves glory in everything (1 Corinthians 10:31) since the beginning of time. God has promised to never leave us nor forsake us (Deuteronomy 31:6), and sometimes His provision comes in the form of a Craigslist find or a great deal at the store.

Scholarships, grants, and loans

When our family was living on a low income, our church awarded our family a scholarship to attend several classes and retreats. A local MOPS (Mothers of Preschoolers) club waived part of my yearly dues, and our preschool gave us a partial tuition credit. When we decided to use cloth diapers because we couldn't afford to diaper two children at once, the Cloth Diaper

Foundation granted us a loan. This now-defunct nonprofit sent all cloth diapering supplies needed to low-income families with the requirement that they send them back or pass them along to others in need. (Two other similar organizations—the Rebecca Foundation's Cloth Diaper Closet and Giving Diapers, Giving Hope—are in operation as of this writing.)

I admit that it wasn't easy to ask for help or even admit we needed it. Most of us have no qualms about applying for college scholarships, yet we shy away from requesting financial aid for other things.

There's a fine balance, though, in asking for help. Here is where knowing whether you have an income problem or a spending problem comes into play. If you have a spending problem and can't afford the event you want to attend, school tuition, or club dues, then it would be wise to rework your budget and cut back on unnecessary spending to make room for the things you desire.

But if you have an income problem, you should have no second thoughts about applying for aid. Yes, it's easier to be on the giving side, but don't rob generous donors of the blessing of giving to *you*. Accept the help. Look at it as God's provision, and thank Him for it.

Kisses from Jesus

I spent my first year after college teaching the children of missionaries in Costa Rica. It was 2003, and the internet and smart phones hadn't yet become part of everyday life. Communication with my family and friends back in North Carolina was limited. Familiar smells and tastes of home took on extraordinary meaning.

One night I wrote in my journal, *I just want some spaghetti. I like rice and beans and fruit and cheese, but it seems like we eat some combination of the four for every meal.*

I had just finished writing when my host mother called to me from the bottom of the stairway which led to my one-room apartment.

"Errrin! La cena está lista!" *Dinner is ready!*

As I walked down the steps, a familiar aroma wafted toward me. *Spaghetti?* My host mom had made *spaghetti*! I took my seat at the table, and she placed a huge plate of pasta and red sauce in front of me. It wasn't my mom's spaghetti, but it was spaghetti nonetheless.

Call it a coincidence if you like, but I saw it as God's provision. He knew my needs, and on that day it was my homesick heart that begged for a little pick-me-up. His provision came as a plate of pasta made with love by a Costa Rican woman accustomed to cooking rice and beans. My Costa Rican mom had never made spaghetti before, and she never made it again, but it met my need that night.

After that incident, my American roommate and I began calling these little blips of God's provision "kisses from Jesus." They were things we could've easily overlooked or chalked up to happenstance, but they pointed us to God instead. Learning to recognize God's presence in these ordinary blessings would prove helpful when, nearly a decade later, it was the little "kisses from Jesus" that got us through each day.

FIGHTING PRIDE TO ACCEPT HELP

I didn't mind accepting a plate of spaghetti that night, but years later, I found it more difficult to receive blessings from others. When I was old enough to provide for myself, I hid my government-issued WIC food checks from family and friends and struggled with letting others know we were barely making it. We were afraid, ashamed, embarrassed.

Each spring, the women's ministry at our church planned a retreat. I wanted so badly to attend. I longed to form friendships with the other women, but there was no way we could scrounge up a couple hundred dollars to cover the cost. Then, one Sunday the pastor announced that there were a select number of scholarships available for women who couldn't afford the fee.

I was filled with hope and excitement at the possibility of attending the retreat, but my emotions took a nosedive when he told us how to apply for one of the scholarships: you had to visit the ministry table and write your name on a sign-up sheet. As much as I wanted to attend the event, I couldn't bear the shame of writing my name on that paper for all to see. *What if one of the ladies with whom I desired friendship sees my name written there? Or worse—what if someone sees me at the table, signing up? Would these ladies take pity on me and offer friendship based solely on that pity? That would be even worse than the embarrassment of not being able to afford the retreat.*

Will knew of my hesitation, but he still encouraged me to request a scholarship. After the service, I stood at a distance from the table and waited for a moment when no one was around so I could quickly slide over and jot down my name. The moment never came. When we left church that day, I had resolved not to attend the retreat. Later, at Will's continued prompting, I emailed the women's ministry director, told her we were living on a low income and could use a scholarship. She was delighted to bless me with it.

The retreat turned out to be a gift from the Lord that I almost missed because of my pride. Later, I received scholarships to attend two more retreats at that church. At the second one, I was shocked to learn that one of my roommates, a single mom of teenagers, was also enjoying the event as a gift from the congregation. When she confided her struggles to me and our other roommate, I felt a wave of relief wash over me, and I was able to share freely about my own challenges.

"I thought we were the only ones," I confessed.

"No," she said, shaking her head. "You never know who around you is struggling."

IT'S NOT EASY TO ASK

As I was conducting interviews for this book, a pattern among women of my generation became clear. We don't like to ask for help.

The Riccis, our Canadian friends whom I introduced in chapter 3, were accustomed to blessing others financially before they ran into financial trouble themselves. In fact, during a three-month missionary stint in Tanzania when they were newlyweds, they met a young man they ended up supporting through his first year of college.

"We gave him our savings," Beth said. "$4,000."

But when it came to their own financial needs, they felt ashamed. The Canadian government subsidizes all families with children, and the lower the income, the more aid the family receives, Beth explained. But in their most desperate moments, even this wasn't enough. Embarrassed to share their situation with family and friends, the Riccis secretly secured groceries at a food bank on two separate occasions. Beth described the time as both "humiliating and frustrating."

Eventually the Riccis realized their loved ones wanted to help. After confiding in their close friends, someone brought them bananas and diapers. Another anonymous person left $100 in an envelope on their porch. Beth now sees that time in their lives as faith-building, her personal manna in a wilderness season.

"We knew God cared about the very smallest and tangible needs in our lives," she said. "Those needs weren't always met how we expected, but they were always met in the end."

Many of the families I interviewed entered their season of financial struggle feeling ashamed to ask for help, but once they did, they experienced the blessing of God's provision in a way they might not have experienced if they had remained quiet. Delilah, one of my readers who is a stay-at-home mom in North Carolina, has watched her family face financial hardship for more than eight years now. She believes they wouldn't have made it without the help of others. "Find encouragement and support," she said. "Don't be ashamed and try to do it alone."

When our friends Mike and Megan returned to the United States after serving as international missionaries for three years, they found it difficult to secure employment. The couple decided to selectively share their needs with friends and family. "It's a very humbling place to be," Megan said. She encourages those in crisis to be open with others. "Be transparent with those who care about you, work hard at whatever is put in front of you, and ask for help."

Our friends Austin and Keelie, who live in Texas, have witnessed God's provision for their family and countless others, as they struggled on a low income while Austin worked as a pastor and Keelie helped run a food pantry. "We were trying to sell our old house, so we were paying two house payments for about a year," Austin said. "It got tough. We ate a *lot* of beans and rice that year. We got to a point where we could've used some of those bags of food that Keelie and her team were putting together each week, but we were afraid of what that would communicate if one of the pastors, who was being paid by the church, was getting food from the church's food pantry."

Fast forward five years to when Austin became the executive director at another food pantry. This pantry operated with an open-door policy where the only requirement was that recipients live in the same county as the facility. "The culture of the pantry was, 'If you feel like you need help, we'll provide it,'" Austin said. "It removed any potential stigma that comes along with seeking help."

Keelie advises those who are struggling to not wait to request aid. "It's better to get assistance before you hit complete bill crisis," she says. "If you genuinely need help, then it's important you find it."

It's also important to note that many people still encounter blessings when they are silent about their struggles. God's provision is just as meaningful when we are silent, but it may come more quickly, be more consistent, or be more overt when we seek help.

Delilah, Mike and Megan, Austin and Keelie—like my family—are not alone. I spoke with families all over North America who have found God's provision in extra work hours, anonymous checks, hand-me-down clothing and household goods, and more. When you feel like you're *just barely making it*, it can be hard to see past the difficulties and recognize God's provision in your life. These families reminded me that God provides in both big and small ways. *Recognizing* His provision is half the battle.

WHAT DOES THE BIBLE SAY ABOUT SEEKING HELP?

Some people think God does not like to be troubled with our constant coming and asking. The way to trouble God is not to come at all.

DWIGHT L. MOODY

It's humbling to admit when we are in need, but it can also bring us closer to God and help us recognize and praise His provision in our lives. In fact, God's Word encourages us to ask for help when we need it. Psalm 121:1–2 says, "I lift my eyes up to the mountains—where does my help come from? My help comes from the LORD, the Maker of heaven and earth." In one of my favorite Scriptures, the apostle Paul tells the church at Philippi, "Do not be anxious about anything, but in every situation, by prayer and petition, with thanksgiving, present your requests to God" (Philippians 4:6). In Galatians 6:2, Paul admonishes believers in Christ to "carry each other's burdens." Later, in verse 10, he writes, "As we have opportunity, let us do good to all people, especially to those who belong to the family of believers." In Romans 12:13, Paul encourages the church to "Share with the Lord's people who are in need. Practice hospitality."

The book of Acts shows believers sharing their possessions with each other to the point that no one is in need. These early Christians operated under the belief that their belongings weren't theirs, but God's. In chapter 4, verses 32 through 35, Luke writes:

> No one claimed that any of their possessions was their own, but they shared everything they had. With great power the apostles continued to testify to the resurrection of the Lord Jesus. And God's grace was so powerfully at work in them all that there were no needy persons among them. For from time to time those who owned land or houses sold them, brought the money from the sales and put it at the apostles' feet, and it was distributed to anyone who had need.

In what is arguably the wealthiest and most prosperous culture that's ever existed, it's rare for Western Christians to operate this way. But God's Word is rife with encouragement to be generous. In 2 Corinthians 9:6–7 and 10–12, Paul writes:

> Whoever sows sparingly will also reap sparingly, and whoever sows generously will also reap generously. Each of you should give what you have decided in your heart to give, not reluctantly or under compulsion, for God loves a cheerful giver . . . Now he who supplies seed to the sower and bread for food will also supply and increase your store of seed and will enlarge the harvest of your righteousness. You will be enriched in every way so that you can be generous on every occasion, and through us your generosity will result in thanksgiving to God.
>
> This service that you perform is not only supplying the needs of the Lord's people but is also overflowing in many expressions of thanks to God.

When God's people help others, they're demonstrating His love and kindness. When we receive provision from other people, we're able to witness God's generosity in *our* lives and praise *Him*. Both giver and recipient can worship God together, knowing the only one who deserves glory is God himself, who gives everything to everyone as He determines (Proverbs 16:9).

EVERY GIFT IS FROM GOD

Every good and perfect gift is from above, coming down from the Father of the heavenly lights, who does not change like shifting shadows.

JAMES 1:17

Western culture teaches that if we work hard, we will reap the benefits of that hard work. Likewise, God's Word encourages a strong work ethic and speaks of rewarding those who are good stewards of their time and talents. Proverbs 10:4–5 says, "Lazy hands make for poverty, but diligent hands bring wealth. He who gathers crops in summer is a prudent son, but he who sleeps during harvest is a disgraceful son." In chapter 13, we'll look at how you can put your gifts to use and create more income for your family. While I don't disagree with the notion of working hard in order to achieve your dreams and provide for your loved ones, I fear we've taken things to an extreme and too often applaud our own efforts instead of giving God credit for providing for our needs.

Yes, we are His instruments. Yes, He has given us gifts to use to bring Him glory *and* to provide for our families, but it *all* comes from Him, my friends. When we forget that, we come dangerously close to adopting a humanistic worldview. God's Word reminds us that *everything* we have comes from the Lord. Romans 11:36 says, "For from him and through him and for him are all things. To him be the glory forever! Amen." If we are not careful, pride can take root in our lives, and we can begin to operate out of the false belief that success is the result of our own merits. I know that was the case with me, although I would never have admitted it or even seen it in myself before our season of low-income living. It took a humbling, a knocking down of the pride that ran deeper than we knew, for us to realize that everything we have comes from God alone.

When we live by the philosophy that we have earned and are entitled to our possessions, we're more likely to hold onto them tightly rather than share them freely. When we remember that all things come from the Lord, it's easier to hold His blessings with open hands and give generously.

THE SPIRITUAL DISCIPLINE
OF GRATITUDE

Eucharisteo—thanksgiving—always precedes the miracle.

ANN VOSKAMP

Just last week, as I was sudsing up my little girls' hair with pricey shampoo, I began to worship the Lord with thanksgiving for all He has provided for our family. You see, my friend, I got that shampoo free with store credits I earned by blogging. I remember a time when I made my own natural shampoo. I didn't want to expose my babies to the toxins found in many cheaper shampoos, but there was no way we could afford the more expensive natural brands. I diluted castile soap and used it as shampoo. It wasn't tear-free; I had to be especially careful around my little ones' eyes. Still, it did the job. Now, here I am years later, using one of the top shampoo brands out there, and it leads me to worship because I know it's from God.

It was such a simple thing, something I could've easily over-looked. I disregarded everyday occurrences like this for years. If we had never gone through a season of want, I don't know if I would see something as minor as shampoo as the Lord's provision. But now that I do, I ask Him to help me not to forget, to help me cultivate gratitude in everything, in seasons of want and in seasons of plenty.

The apostle Paul practiced this well. Near the end of his letter to the church in Philippi, he wrote:

I have learned to be content whatever the circumstances. I know what it is to be in need, and I know what it is to have plenty. I have learned the secret of being content in any and every situation, whether well fed or hungry, whether living in plenty or in want. I can do all this through him who gives me strength. (Philippians 4:11–13)

Everything we own—from persimmons to shampoo—is God's provision. When we remember that all things come from the Lord, it enables us to practice contentment in every season. We can practice the spiritual discipline of gratitude as we wash our children's hair, as we clean our homes, as we prepare meals for our families—for God has given us these children, these roofs over our heads, the very food on our tables. We can sit outside our sprawling Southern mansions or tiny city apartments and praise God for meeting our every need. Practicing gratitude in each small gesture will help you go from a mental and emotional state of "just barely making it" to *more than just making it*—if you let it.

For gratitude stills discontentment.

ELEVEN

THE ELEPHANT IN THE CHURCH:

The Government Aid Question

Let each of you look not only to his own interests, but also to the interests of others.

PHILIPPIANS 2:4 (ESV)

FALL 2010

I checked our mailbox every day for what seemed like an eternity. In actuality it was probably only a week before I turned the key to the little gray box and found a letter inside from the Department of Social Services. I wanted to rip into it right away, but I closed the mailbox first, locked it, and looked around to make sure none of my neighbors were watching. *Oh, God, if only the answer is "yes,"* I prayed silently. *We'll be able to eat so much better, so much more. Is this how You will provide?*

I stepped away from the mailboxes and into a grassy clearing. I turned over the long white envelope with trembling hands and finally tore it open. I slowly unfolded the letter and began reading.

I only had to read a few lines before I realized the news wasn't what I'd been expecting. We were barely making it, yet the letter stated we had *not qualified* for food stamps! When I looked at the figures, it was clear that I had applied during a month when I'd earned significantly more at my freelancing job than I did normally. They had based our eligibility on those numbers. In an instant, I went from feeling shame about applying for aid—of not even wanting a neighbor to see the envelope—to disappointment over being rejected by the system that was supposed to help us.

My morale plummeted; I stifled tears. My favorite season had produced a colorful vista of landscaping in our neighborhood, and I noticed a few red, orange, and yellow leaves that had valready fallen to the ground. I reached down to pick them up instead of crunching them beneath my feet, thinking our little girl might like to do some sketches with them. I walked back to our townhouse and gingerly opened the back door. I didn't want Will to notice my watery eyes. I had convinced him we needed to apply for foods stamps even though he had hesitated. If this was a bruise to my pride, it would leave a gaping wound in his. I reached down to hand our toddler the leaves I had gathered, and she squealed in delight. Our newborn was sleeping peacefully in her baby swing, oblivious that her family was in need, as she was warm and cozy and well fed. I took the letter out of my pocket as I entered the kitchen, unfolded it, and lay it on the counter, steeling my expression as I gave Will the news.

"They rejected us."

A GENERATION IN NEED

Even after we reached the point of admitting we needed help, we still felt guilty about using government aid. Accepting assistance wasn't just a taboo topic in the church; it was something many people looked down on.

However, with unemployment and foreclosure rates rising just as those born in the 1980s were entering adulthood, not to mention the masses graduating from college with mountains of debt, people who never dreamed of accepting welfare found themselves standing in line to request some kind of relief. That was the case for our family. Applying for food stamps felt like a final straw. We'd already been using government resources for nearly a year.

Nine months earlier, I'd been lonely. We had joined a church but had developed only a few friendships. When my sister told me about a free community play group, I embraced the opportunity. I didn't know the group was government-funded.

It wasn't long before I discovered another program the group offered: Parent Educator Mentors. These mentors would visit homes once a month and give families parenting advice. Our firstborn was a toddler, and I was floundering. The prospect of an older woman, a mentor, visiting us was exciting. I needed a friend.

During each meeting our mentor, Marnie, played games and read books with our daughter, all while teaching me about developmental milestones and family well-being. I began to open up to Marnie about our financial hardships. Marnie ended up being a life raft when I was just barely making it as a wife, mom, and homemaker. She was one of the first people to learn we were expecting our second baby—the baby whose name would mean "pearl." That surprise daughter would become *our* pearl, born in the midst of a dirty oyster-shell time of our lives. Even before our financial counselor, Randy, told us we had an income problem, Marnie advised that we needed help.

While our toddler played with an *If You Give a Mouse a*

Cookie game on the living room floor one day, Marnie and I began talking about the pregnancy.

"Are you excited?" she asked.

"Yes, but I'm a little stressed because I don't know how we will make it," I said. "We already feel so strained. We have health insurance, but I'm still worried about paying medical bills."

"Erin, you probably qualify for Medicaid for pregnant moms," Marnie offered. "Have you ever looked into that?"

I hadn't even heard of Medicaid for pregnant moms, and I didn't know much about Medicaid itself, except that it was government-funded health insurance. "No, I've never looked into it," I said. "I figured we didn't qualify for government programs."

We aren't poor, are we? I wondered to myself. Will and I had traveled to many impoverished nations on mission trips both individually before we were married and together as newlyweds. I knew how *true poverty* looked. Sure, we struggled, but we were renting a comfortable townhouse, had plenty of clothing, and although things were difficult, God met our every need. I didn't comprehend the inadequacy of our income or how much more financial anxiety we would experience in the coming years.

"Erin, I'm only asking because I want to help you," Marnie said. "How much money does Will bring home each month?"

I told her the amount, speaking slowly and resolutely, adding, "I also bring in anywhere from an extra $60 to $200 per month with my side jobs."

Surely this doesn't deem us eligible to receive aid, does it? I thought to myself.

"Erin, with your family size—and especially expecting another baby—you're living around poverty level. No wonder you feel like you're just barely making it. You don't have enough money to live on. You need help." Marnie spoke carefully, as if she didn't want to offend me. "Yes, you would definitely qualify, and Medicaid should even retroactively cover what you've already paid. You need to apply immediately. I can help you with the application."

I felt my cheeks grow warm.

"It's OK, Erin." Marnie patted my hand. "Don't be embarrassed. The government set up these programs to help people in true need. That's your family right now."

Looking back, I was drowning in both emotional and financial turmoil at the time the Lord put Marnie in my life. God used her and others to help us get back on our feet, to go from barely surviving to more than just making it. Wherever *you* are right now, dear reader, I know He can do the same for *you*.

PRIDE EXPOSED

Medicaid was a godsend. It covered everything our primary insurance did not. We told my parents but otherwise kept the fact that we were on welfare strictly secret. The people in my social circles looked down upon those who accepted government aid, or at least I imagined they did. We thought we were the only ones, so we told no one. I worried that doctors would treat me differently if they saw "Medicaid" on my paperwork. If it ever came up, I stuck to my well-rehearsed story: "We've fallen on hard times. My husband is a teacher with his master's degree, but the state of North Carolina doesn't pay teachers well. I work odd jobs from home. We have a house in another state that we can't sell. We have always paid our taxes. We just need a little help right now to get us through a hard time. We aren't lazy. We are hard workers."

THE STIGMA AND THE SHAME

I was ashamed, thinking anyone who discovered our secret would think poorly of us, that we were scamming the system, that we were to be pitied. My understanding of government aid expanded as I got older, but feelings of shame lingered, leftovers from the ideas I had absorbed as part of a subculture which, I now believe, is largely misinformed about how government aid works and how it helps those in need. It was during a conversation with some of my husband's seminary classmates that I first realized these programs exist.

When Will was in seminary, I envied the seminary wives who could stay home with their kids. The only way we could afford seminary was because he was working part-time and I was teaching full-time; we didn't yet have children. There was one other student whose wife also worked. They had one son in daycare. We became friends, and one night over dinner, the couple began telling us about their neighbors.

"They bring us extra milk," they said, laughing. "They get, like, twenty gallons a month!"

"I don't understand." I was puzzled. "Where do they get this milk?"

"They're on government aid," the wife snickered. "Here we are, working our butts off so people like them can stay home and raise their children. I don't mind taking the free milk because our tax dollars are paying for their food."

"That is so not fair!" I exclaimed. "I wish I didn't have to work. It sounds like they're just taking advantage of our hard work."

As I share this memory with you here, I'm seared with shame that I took part in that conversation. My lack of understanding about government aid and my assumptions about those who used it showed both my naiveté and my sense of privilege. Little did I know that our family would one day benefit from the WIC program (Aid for Women, Infants, and Children), which provides nutritious food to ensure the health of low-income pregnant and nursing mothers and their children. When we were on welfare, I thought back to that conversation frequently. I prayed that those friends—that all of our friends—would never find out we were now the ones using their tax dollars to cover our health expenses and feed our family. I relate well to author Donald Miller's description of his first time witnessing someone using food stamps:[1]

> The lady in front of me pulled out food stamps to pay for her groceries. I had never seen food stamps before. They were more colorful than I imagined and looked more like money than stamps. It was obvious as she unfolded the currency that she, I, and the checkout girl were quite uncomfortable with the interaction. I wished there was something I could do. I wished I could pay for her groceries myself, but to do so would have been to cause a greater scene. The checkout girl quickly performed her job, signing and verifying a few documents, then filed the lady through the line. The woman never lifted her head as she organized her bags of groceries and set them into her cart. She walked away from the checkout stand in the sort of stiff movements a person uses when they know they are being watched.
>
> On the drive over the mountain that afternoon, I realized that it was not the woman who should be pitied; it was me. Somehow I had come to believe that because a person is in need, they are candidates for sympathy, not just charity. It

was not that I wanted to buy her groceries; the government was already doing that. I wanted to buy her dignity. And yet, by judging her, I was the one taking her dignity away.

When I came to understand that some people truly need government aid to live, my emotions ran the gamut from judgment to pity. Confusing this pity with compassion, I stripped those on welfare of their dignity, just as Donald Miller did—just like many of us do without even realizing it. Then, in what felt like one fell swoop, I became one of them. Now I was the one standing naked.

FEET IN TWO WORLDS

Hiding the fact that we were on welfare made me feel like we were living a lie. I had prided myself on being authentic, transparent. But this was something I felt like I could tell no one.

Thankfully, I rarely heard anyone I knew mock people who were living on a low income. But I found myself becoming sensitive to social media posts and comments pertaining to government aid. We were in the middle of a recession, and while many Americans were struggling in secret, judgmental attitudes from those who were not prevailed. It wasn't uncommon for me to see posts wherein friends complained about people on government aid using their hard-earned tax dollars. Often, these posts and comments implied that people on welfare refuse to work. This wasn't the case for our family or for many people I met while I sat waiting in the WIC office each month, but I remained silent.

Once, I came up with a pseudonym to comment on a heated thread in an online parenting forum. The original poster complained about the poor having too many babies.

"If you can't support them, don't get pregnant," she wrote.

Late at night and hidden behind the protective wall of my computer screen, hot tears streamed down my cheeks. I swallowed my sobs, afraid of waking Will or the girls. My shame quickly escalated into anger. I cradled my newborn in the crook of my left elbow as I typed a reply: "And why *shouldn't* the poor have a right to have children? Why *should* only those with money be entitled to reproduce? I don't believe in relying on government aid for life, but what if a couple is going through financial crisis during their childbearing years? Should they be shamed? Mocked? Sterilized because they don't have money?"

Later, I felt conflicted for engaging the stranger—a random, nameless person on the internet whom I would never meet. Yet, to me, this person represented the world, my world—or my former world, at least. She represented the world of the "haves", a world of privilege. I had lived in that world, and now we were planted firmly on the other side, in the world of the "have-nots", a world of need, a world filled with those desperate for help, and sadly, a world in which some people deemed us unworthy of basic human rights like reproduction. *If we ever make it through this time*, I told myself, *I want to change the mindsets of my peers, to do all I can to remove the stigma and the shame of the poor.*

CAN I JUST RUN AND HIDE?

In the meantime, I lived in fear that someone would recognize me while I was using my WIC checks in the grocery store or see me walk into the Department of Social Services building for one of our visits. I learned which grocery stores to frequent and which ones to avoid. More than once, I encountered a cashier who didn't know how to process WIC checks. I wanted to crawl under the conveyor belt whenever he or she would call over the loud speaker, "Price check on WIC item! Price check on WIC item!" I couldn't get out of the store fast enough.

When I ran into someone I knew, I hid my checks and pushed the cart around the store for a few minutes after our interaction before leaving without my groceries. There was no way I would use WIC in front of someone I knew. I could only imagine what they would think or what rumors they might start.

If ever I saw another mom using WIC or food stamps, though, it was as if we had an unspoken bond, a camaraderie of sorts. A weight lifted because I knew I wasn't alone. Instead of hiding my checks, I held them outside my purse, more visible for the other woman to see. I made eye contact and smiled. I wanted her to know she wasn't alone. Knowing we were walking this road with others restored some dignity.

NOT ALONE

The longer we stayed on WIC and Medicaid, the more I came to realize that my feelings of shame were fueled by pride. I felt alone, yet I was surrounded by low-income people. I was living in a world of which I had little prior knowledge, a world I had stereotyped and misjudged.

Because we were on WIC, I had to take the girls for regular health checkups. I would tell them we were going to the doctor; I never wanted them to mention the "WIC office" to someone else. Though I worried someone would see my car in the parking lot, once we were inside, I relaxed. It was just me and my fellow government aid recipients in the waiting room. We were all in this together. Years went by before I discovered that one of my best friends had been on both Medicaid and WIC too. Neither of us had been brave enough to share our struggles until we were past them.

One day I ran into another mom from my local MOPS group. We didn't speak, except to say "Hi." *She's on WIC too?* I was shocked. We both smiled sheepishly. We both looked down and then into each other's eyes. We both knew. We both held a secret. And we would keep it for each other. We would tell no one, for to share that we had seen each other at the WIC office would implicate us.

THE SHAME IS NOT ISOLATED

Years later, when I finally began to share our story, I learned that I was far from alone in my shame. I've discussed the government aid dilemma with hundreds of women, and not a single one told me she didn't feel some apprehension or judgment for using WIC checks, food stamps, Medicaid, or some other form of assistance.

May, a pastor's wife and working mother of four in Maine, spoke to me about the humiliation she and her husband felt when using food stamps and WIC. "Even if the help of the state was temporary, we felt right away that we became the statistic of those taking advantage of everyone around us because we had to rely on taxpayers," she said. "Every time we would check out, we would hang our heads low, hoping that the cashier wouldn't notice that we didn't have a bank debit card."

When May used her WIC checks, she would strategically wait to pick a line with no one else waiting. "It lessened the shame," she said. "Until, of course, the cashier didn't know how to process the checks. I would soon find out who was quick to do the checkout, and I would go to that cashier each time I had to use the checks."

Despite her strong faith, May felt conflicted about her family's use of government aid. "I believed this whole time (that) God was our Provider. He was and still is, but I couldn't see that this was His way of providing for our family at the time," she said. "I saw it as a punishment of some sort—to shame us. It's amazing how influential opinions are until you, yourself, become the person in need. Then what? Guilt and shame follow. No support. Just judging eyes. Yep, the pastor and his family were on government food stamps and WIC."

I spoke with several foster parents who experienced the same stigma when using WIC checks, even when their own families weren't living on a low income. Foster children automatically qualify for WIC, and the government encourages foster families to use this resource to cut down on the costs of raising children.

Ashleigh, a Florida mom of three foster-adopted children, who has two other children, chose to use WIC checks to pay for the expensive infant formula she needed to nourish the babies she fostered. Like me and May, she chose to visit stores during off hours and only once a month so she was less likely to run into people who might say something judgmental to her. "Even with that, I found it to be much less awkward when people would just ask about our situation, and I could choose to explain the parts of it I wanted to," she said. "People often responded much differently once they knew we were fostering the kids we were buying stuff for."

Although Ashleigh's family has chosen to no longer use WIC because they are financially able to provide for the children they have now adopted, they still use Medicaid. "I'm grateful for it because, without it, honestly, we couldn't have adopted [our son with a heart defect]," Ashleigh said. "His medical bills are just too much."

Monica, a North Carolina mom of four foster-adopted children, also feels uncomfortable using WIC checks at the grocery store based on how she used to view WIC recipients herself. "I always feel the need to tell people we have foster kids," she said. "I think I feel so judged when I use [WIC checks] because I used to work in a grocery store and judged people who would pay with them."

Becoming a foster parent has given Monica a whole new perspective. Instead of judging those who use government aid, Monica now realizes that everyone has a reason they are living with assistance, and it's not her place to judge.

HOW DOES GOVERNMENT AID WORK?

There are many government programs to help struggling families. Some are for the poorest of the poor, but others are available for those who need short-term help due to job loss, illness, or temporary homelessness. Some programs are stigmatized more than others.

The United States has set up a safety net to provide for the basic needs of its citizens. Taxpayers fund this system, with the security that they can benefit in the event that they fall on hard times.

While I've included the most widely-used programs, this list isn't comprehensive. You can learn more at benefits.gov.

Medicaid

Medicaid is government-funded health insurance for the poor. Several different programs fall under the branch of Medicaid—Medicaid for pregnant women, children, the disabled, seniors, individuals, and CHIP. We'll briefly explore each of these. For more in-depth information, visit medicaid.gov.

Medicaid for pregnant women is available to women through their first six weeks postpartum. Women within a certain income bracket who aren't insured can qualify for full benefits, which cover all pregnancy and delivery expenses. Those who have primary insurance, as we did, can use Medicaid as a supplement if they still fall within income qualifications. As supplemental insurance, Medicaid will cover expenses that primary insurance doesn't cover.

Medicaid for children can function as primary or secondary insurance. When our family was using these programs, any child born to a mother on Medicaid qualified for a full year of Medicaid. While the program varies by state, it usually covers most or all medical expenses. Foster children automatically receive benefits, and many states continue this coverage until age eighteen, even after children are adopted.

Medicaid for the disabled provides health coverage to more than ten million children and adults with disabilities.[2] Some states automatically award benefits to pre-term infants due to potential developmental issues resulting from premature birth.

Medicaid for seniors acts as a supplemental insurance to Medicare, which is a federal health insurance program for people age sixty-five and older. All seniors, regardless of income, qualify for Medicare once they turn sixty-five, but only those with low incomes can benefit from Medicaid. Medicaid can help low-income seniors pay their Medicare premiums and any out-of-pocket expenses Medicare doesn't cover.

Medicaid for individuals is difficult to qualify for unless you have an *extremely* low income. Eligibility varies per state, but most adults under age sixty-five don't receive Medicaid.

The Children's Health Insurance Program (CHIP) is another government-funded health insurance program for children. Children whose parents' income might not qualify them for Medicaid might still be eligible for CHIP. CHIP might require a small premium and some co-pays.

Food programs

Food stamps/EBT

The food stamps program provides monetary allotments on Electronic Benefit Transfer (EBT) cards for low-income individuals and families. Food stamps don't cover tobacco, pet food, paper products, toiletries, or alcohol. EBT cards look and work the same as debit cards, which helps maintain a sense of dignity for those who might feel embarrassed using stamps.

Eligibility varies per state and is determined by both income and family size. Most states also require that food stamp recipients not have excessive savings. As of this writing, those with combined savings and checking bank balances over $2,001 cannot receive food stamp benefits in North Carolina—even if they meet other income standards. They must first exhaust any savings to under $2,000 to qualify. The number is higher—to a combined bank balance of no more than $3,001—for families who share a household with anyone over age sixty or with a disability.[3]

WIC (Women, Infants, and Children)

The WIC program provides specific foods, baby formula, nutritional education, and breastfeeding support to pregnant and nursing women, infants, and children up to age five. WIC support includes certain health tests and referrals. When I had WIC, the WIC nurse routinely screened my children and me for anemia. She also weighed and measured my children to ensure proper growth.

Unlike food stamps, which allow recipients to choose their own foods, WIC has very specific guidelines. WIC foods include infant formula, cereals, juice, eggs, milk, cheese, peanut butter, beans, bread or tortillas, canned fish, baby foods, soy and tofu products for vegetarians, and produce.

WIC eligibility is dependent on income and family size, with exact guidelines varying per state. WIC recipients must also be determined to be at risk of malnutrition. At the time I received WIC, having a low income was considered a nutritional risk. Not everyone who meets eligibility may receive WIC, as Congress only allots a certain number of funds to the program each year.[4]

At this writing, many WIC programs still issue paper checks to recipients, but, by October 2020, the government has mandated that all states issue benefits on EBT cards instead. I had to use paper checks when I had WIC, and it was incredibly humiliating to pay this way at the check-out line in stores. No one *should* feel shame using WIC, but these outdated, highly visible methods are another subtle way that people on aid can feel marginalized and have to jump through hoops, even at the supermarket.

How to Apply for Medicaid/EBT/WIC

The best way to discover if you're eligible for these programs is through your state's Department of Social Services website. Check for income eligibility and what documents you'll need to apply. Some offices allow walk-ins; others require scheduled appointments.

National School Lunch Program (NSLP)

NSLP provides lunches to low-income children attending public schools. Some qualify for free lunches, while others receive them at a reduced rate. NSLP also includes free or reduced breakfasts in some states.

Children whose parents are receiving other types of benefits, such as food stamps, may automatically qualify for NSLP in some states. Schools send home applications at the beginning of each school year, but parents can apply any time by requesting an application from the school.[5]

Unemployment Benefits

Unemployment benefits pay workers who have lost their jobs. Those who qualify receive a portion of their wages through this program. High rates of unemployment since the Great Recession have made this one of the most socially acceptable forms of government aid.

An individual may obtain unemployment benefits for a limited amount of time, although the government can extend this period during times of nationwide crisis. During the recession, the government extended this period from twenty-six weeks to ninety-nine weeks.[6] Each state sets its own unemployment eligibility requirements. Apply through your state's unemployment insurance office.

AN ATTITUDE ADJUSTMENT

> This is how we know what love is: Jesus Christ laid down his life for us. And we ought to lay down our lives for our brothers and sisters. If anyone has material possessions and sees a brother or sister in need but has no pity on them, how can the love of God be in that person? Dear children, let us not love with words or speech but with actions and in truth. (1 John 3:16–18)

For years, I've listened to my peers complain about those living on government aid (and I've done some complaining myself), yet I've seldom heard an argument against welfare that is rooted in Scripture. As I battled my own hesitations about accepting assistance, reading what the Bible says about poverty, charity, and our relationship with the government helped me view the topic in a completely different light. If you study Scripture, it doesn't take long to discover that God's Word is brimming with admonitions to care for the poor. God's love for the poor is clear. Proverbs 14:31 says, "Whoever oppresses the poor shows contempt for their Maker, but whoever is kind to the needy honors God." Those are pretty strong words.

You might be thinking, "But I don't oppress the poor!" I didn't think I did either. But what is the definition of "oppress"? Learning Dictionary defines it two ways: "to treat a person or group of people in a cruel or unfair way" and "to make someone feel sad or worried for a long period of time."[7] While none of us may be actively "oppressing" those living on a lower income than we are, doesn't our lack of compassion and support count as a sort of "oppression"? I think it might. At the same time, Scripture describes kindness to the poor as honoring to God. This should encourage us. When Moses reiterated the laws the Israelites were to follow, he included strong admonitions about caring for the poor:

> If anyone is poor among your fellow Israelites in any of the towns in the land the LORD your God is giving you, do not be hardhearted or tightfisted toward them. Rather, be openhanded and freely lend them whatever they need. Be careful not to harbor this wicked thought: "The seventh year, the year for canceling debts, it near," so that you do not show ill will toward the needy among your fellow Israelites and give them nothing. They may then appeal to the LORD against you, and you will be found guilty of sin. Give generously to them and do so without a grudging heart; then because of this the LORD your God will bless you in all your work and in everything you put your hand to. There will always be poor people in the land. Therefore I command

you to be openhanded toward your fellow Israelites who
are poor and needy in your land. (Deuteronomy 15:7–11)

Because this passage refers to treating the citizens of the
country at hand (Israel) a certain way, some have interpreted
this as meaning we don't have to treat poor immigrants with the
same giving spirit as we do fellow nationals. But we must look
at the entirety of Scripture before drawing conclusions. Indeed,
in Leviticus 19:33–34, Moses wrote, "When a foreigner resides
among you in your land, do not mistreat them. The foreigner
residing among you must be treated as your native-born. Love
them as yourself, for you were foreigners in Egypt. I am the
LORD your God."

The New Testament shares this same message. As I included
in chapter 10, in Acts 4:32–35, we see the believers sharing all of
their possessions. No one was in need. Some claim that the Acts
passage shows that Christians are only to care for fellow believers
in need. My friend Allison, a Texas work-at-home mother of five,
has seen this play out in her life.

"If someone needs food, the attitude can be, 'We shouldn't
help them because they made stupid mistakes, or they don't believe
the same way we do,'" she said. "It would be so nice if people
would . . . just help where it's needed." In Matthew 25, Jesus'
story of helping the needy makes no reference to the practice
being exclusive to believers:

"For I was hungry and you gave me something to eat, I was
thirsty and you gave me something to drink, I was a stranger
and you invited me in, I needed clothes and you clothed me,
I was sick and you looked after me, I was in prison and you
came to visit me . . . Truly I tell you, whatever you did for

one of the least of these brothers and sisters of mine, you did for me." (verses 35–36, 40)

Scripture is unmistakably clear: We are to give to those in need. I don't think that all American churches are doing a poor job caring for the needy—the church where Will and I are members places a high priority on caring for our less-fortunate neighbors—but the disdain that many individuals display toward those living on welfare can make it seem that way. Whether perception or reality, this stigma may keep the needy from sharing their struggles with believers who could help.

IT'S THE CHURCH'S RESPONSIBILITY TO CARE FOR THE POOR, NOT THE GOVERNMENT'S

We've established that the Bible is clear about God's heart for the poor and that caring for the needy should be on the forefront of every believer's mind. *But Scripture gives this responsibility to the church, not the government*, you might be thinking.

This is the most common argument I've heard believers make against government aid programs. And I agree that caring for the needy *should* be the church's job. But I like seeing the church work together with programs that are already meeting needs. Some ministries seek out families via the children in their local public school districts, partnering to supply food baskets, clothing, or toys. But when it comes to helping families inquire about aid programs, a stigma remains. When a church cannot afford to feed families, must they send them away hungry? Wouldn't it be better stewardship to partner with programs that are already feeding people? Wouldn't it help break down the shame associated with food stamps, WIC, and Medicaid to have someone from your church help those in need apply for the resources that will ensure they and their children have enough to eat and that their medical needs will be met?

For the same reasons that some claim only the church should care for the poor, we could justify that healing should only come through God. Our Christian culture as a whole welcomes medical treatments, coupled with prayer, for physical healing from illnesses. We see modern medicine as a conduit God uses to care for His people. What if we viewed government aid programs the same way?

Can God use government aid programs to provide for the poor?

I believe God can use anything to meet our needs. I witnessed Him provide for our family through assistance programs. While the Bible doesn't specifically address government aid in America, in Mark 12:17 Jesus instructed the Jews to pay their taxes: "Give back to Caesar what is Caesar's and to God what is God's." Our "Caesar" is our government. When we pay our taxes, our government uses part of the money to care for the poor. That, my friends, makes me thankful to be an American.

My exposé on government aid

We lived with the help of government aid programs for about three years. As we relied on this help through two pregnancies and the infant and toddler years with our girls, I learned to be grateful and chose to look at the help as both a temporary solution and God's provision. Yes, it came from the government, but I believe God has blessed our country. I now look at government aid much differently than I did as a twenty-something with a middle-class income and no children.

I first walked into our local government office with preconceived biases. I bristled at the thought that the workers would assume I was uneducated, lazy, or a scammer of the system. I told myself it was an experiment. I would one day write an exposé on government aid in America. I would write about people abusing the system, about the harsh treatment of the recipients, about the brokenness of the entire program.

I was wrong.

I didn't uncover or confirm any conspiracy theories. Instead, I found a system that ministered to me as well as I would expect the church to do, a system that showered our family with God's love and provision. Even when the government aid workers I met had no intention of doing so, God used them as instruments to break down the hard shell I had placed around my heart. He did it through the unexpected ways He met all our needs. And He did it by tearing down my pride—pride I didn't know existed before I began the humbling journey of living on a low income and surviving with the help of government aid.

TWELVE

CHANGING OUR MINDSETS

Whoever is kind to the poor lends to the LORD,
and he will reward them for what they have done.

PROVERBS 19:17

DECEMBER 2011

I yawned, rubbed my eyes, and stretched my arms. I couldn't shake off my lethargy. The sounds of Big Bird and Cookie Monster echoed from the television, and the faint odor of dirty diaper told me the baby needed changing. I sprang from the couch in a panic. The girls were playing with Little People on the floor, at the base of the sofa where I lay. Obviously, I had fallen asleep, but I had no idea when or for how long. I would have never intentionally taken a nap and left my toddlers to fend for themselves. Something was clearly wrong.

Fatigue had plagued me for several weeks, and I had googled every possible scenario. Yes, I had two active toddlers. I was also in the habit of staying up half the night writing for our local newspaper and my blog, both in an attempt to grow our income. But this didn't feel like normal sleep deprivation.

I fell into bed fully dressed, but late that night I forced myself to put on clean pajamas. As I pulled on my fleece nightshirt, I noticed my stomach was protruding. *I'm never going to lose this baby weight*, I told myself. *But I'm just too tired to exercise. The baby is already a year old, and I still look pregnant.*

Then it hit me. What if I *was* pregnant? Fatigue had been my first sign of pregnancy with both girls. Excitement and fear shot through me. I wanted another child, but I knew Will was right when he said we couldn't afford more. And if I were honest with myself, I was still steeped in depression. Was it postpartum or was it a hopelessness that came from having few friends, a strained marriage, and not enough money to live? I had no idea, but the one thing I did know was that we couldn't bear the expense of one more mouth to feed. I decided to wait until morning to find out if my distended belly was indicative of pregnancy or if I was just bloated. I couldn't sleep, however, so I eventually slid out of bed and quietly unwrapped a pregnancy test.

TWO PINK LINES

I tried to think of a creative way to tell Will the news. As he leaned over to kiss me goodbye at six o'clock the next morning, I whispered, "She has conceived and will bear a son—or a daughter." It was a play on Luke 1:31, which tells the story of how the Virgin Mary would soon conceive Jesus. I thought I was being cute because it was so close to Christmas. But Will was confused.

"What are you talking about?" He pulled back.

"I'm pregnant," I replied, still half asleep.

"I can't deal with this right now," Will said. "I just can't deal with it."

He left for work, and I drifted back to sleep. That day, Will told one person at his school—Kathy, the woman who had brought us groceries. He later confessed that he'd had to hold back tears as he revealed the news. It wasn't that he was sad about having another child. It was that we could barely afford to feed the two we already had. We were in the dark tunnel of low-income living and saw no way out. We felt depleted—emotionally, mentally, financially. Would the Lord somehow restore our joy with this new baby? That was my prayer.

When I called Marilyn to share our news, she said she had wondered if I was pregnant during our meeting with her and Randy a week earlier. She had noticed a little baby bump forming, and she was right. No one knew our financial situation better than Randy and Marilyn, and she encouraged me that nothing took God by surprise; *He* had a plan for this child.

I knew we needed the help of Medicaid again. Our girls still had Medicaid and WIC, but when a baby turns a year old, the mother no longer receives WIC checks. In order to have enough food for a healthy pregnancy, I would also need to be back on WIC. I felt I had no other choice but to drag my two toddlers back into the Department of Social Services to reapply for assistance.

BACK IN THE WIC OFFICE

While I had developed a respectful relationship with several of the WIC workers, an older lady I didn't recognize was processing our application this time. I braced myself, assuming she would judge me. I held on to my pride. I didn't want her to see my fragility, and I didn't want the pity I assumed she would feel. My oldest fidgeted in her seat until I finally placed her in my lap. I balanced one foot on my younger daughter's car seat on the floor, rocking her to sleep. The room was private—just two plain chairs for the girls and me, and a wooden desk with a computer where the intake worker sat.

Absorbed in my own thoughts and trials, I didn't notice the sadness in the worker's eyes until another staff member peeked her head inside the door. "Are you OK, Fran? Want me to take over?"

"No, I've got this," she said. "I can do this. I *need* to do this. Thank you."

Confused, I asked Fran if something was wrong.

"I'm just . . . It's my first day back at work in several weeks," she said, through a tiny pool of tears that she could hold back no longer. "My husband . . . my husband passed away three weeks ago after a short bout with cancer. I need the money, so I had to come back to work as soon as possible. His illness . . . his death . . . it was all very unexpected."

I crumbled. Here I had been so caught up in my own problems that I hadn't noticed this woman's grief. Now that we made eye contact, I could see it. My struggles paled compared to hers. I reached my hand across the desk and patted Fran on the arm. "I'm so sorry. I'm so very sorry. I would love to keep you in my prayers. I am so very sorry for your loss."

Instead of leaving the WIC office feeling defeated and numb that day, the Holy Spirit used that short conversation to shake me alive.

CHANGING MINDSETS

My pride had been slowly deteriorating for more than two years at this point, and I had begun to soften. I had become one of "those people" I had judged all those years earlier. Oddly enough, the very government aid workers I assumed would judge me harshly were the ones God used to soften me. I expected them, of all people, to be bitter toward those who use government aid because they often had to deal with people who abused the system. To my surprise, the ladies who ran my local WIC office were anything but harsh. Instead, they showed me the same kindness I would expect from members of the church.

THE KINDNESS OF STRANGERS

When I went for our WIC visits, I almost always saw the same nurse. Her name was Stephanie, and I felt like we'd become friends of sorts. Since having children, health and wellness had become a passion of mine. Nutrition education was part of our visits, and in the beginning I worried she would think me ignorant. I'll never forget Stephanie reaching out her hand as we talked, looking me in the eyes and restoring my dignity.

"Erin," she said, "this system is designed for people like you." I tried to explain that we weren't abusing the system. I needed to justify our presence there. I felt shame, but I didn't need to. This was another moment the Lord used to open my eyes about how I had wrongly judged others in the same position.

After a while, I started looking forward to my visits. Inside those brick walls I could relax, be myself, stop pretending we were OK when, really, we weren't.

No one but my parents knew we were back on aid, at least at first. Eventually, I would tell others, but mostly only those like us who were also struggling. It came out in bits and pieces, within the context of a shared camaraderie those with sufficient income couldn't understand.

GIVING PEOPLE THE BENEFIT
OF THE DOUBT

Until we embrace our mutual brokenness, our work with low-income people is likely to do more harm than good. I sometimes unintentionally reduce poor people to objects that I use to fulfill my own need to accomplish something. I am not okay, and you are not okay. But Jesus can fix us both.

STEVE CORBETT AND BRIAN FIKKERT,
WHEN HELPING HURTS

Stephanie spoke to me as if I had value. But it wasn't just me she spoke to that way—or at least I hoped it wasn't. I didn't fit the stereotype of the average person on government aid, but what if we as a society, and those of us in the church especially, learned to *never* put anyone in a box, to *never* stereotype, to *never* make assumptions? What if we looked beyond economic situations and stigmas and educational levels and saw the potential for each and every individual? What if we gave people the benefit of the doubt?

"But don't they just abuse the system?" you might ask. "Aren't we the ones paying for it all? Paying for them to eat? Paying for them to birth their babies? Paying for them to have free childcare and cell phones?"

The common belief is that the United States welfare system is riddled with abuse. While I don't deny that there are those who *do* cheat their way through the system, I think we do our fellow human beings a disservice when we assume that the majority of people living with the help of government aid are abusing welfare programs.

The families I met during our time on assistance were mostly hard-working people who had either fallen on hard times or were the working poor—fathers working forty, fifty, or sixty hours per week at low-paying jobs (sometimes multiple jobs) while mothers kept homes and children (some trying to make an income themselves). We must understand that systemic abuse extends beyond those who use government aid and can bleed into many areas. Those from all walks of life and income levels are prone to manipulating the law to benefit themselves personally because we live in a sin-stained, fallen world. Do high-income earners cheat on their taxes? I venture to estimate that many more do than we could ever imagine. Neither the family on government aid under false pretense nor the family finding loopholes for paying their taxes is ethical or excusable. But we should never *assume* someone is in the wrong without knowing the whole story.

JUDGING GROCERY CARTS

I've heard people who view welfare recipients as government moochers say that you can tell from the contents of their grocery carts if they don't really need aid. I can't count the number of times someone has mentioned seeing a person use food stamps to buy steaks or birthday cake, which seems luxurious and unnecessary for those the country has labeled "poor." Couldn't they make the stamps stretch further if they used them for just the basics? There is no doubt they could, but what if you happened to be at the grocery store with that person before a big celebration (like a birthday)? What if he or she just secured a job and decided to celebrate with a steak dinner? Are the poor not entitled to memorialize life's victories and milestones as much as the rich?

I've also heard people say you can tell those who don't deserve government aid by the *other* contents of their grocery carts. For example, someone might have video games or DVDs they pay for with cash, while they pay for all of their food with an EBT card. My friend Melanie, a pastor's wife and mother of five from Mississippi who once lived on welfare herself, pointed out that many of her friends with foster children use WIC checks to buy their food but choose to bless the children under their care with entertainment purchases out of their own pockets. "As a general rule, I think the very safest place for any of us to be is firmly on the side of casting zero judgment," she said. "We never know what's going on in someone else's life."

IT'S HARDER TO CHEAT THAN YOU THINK

Yes, some people do abuse welfare programs. Some illegally sell their EBT cards or WIC checks. Others qualify under false pretenses, using fake bank statements or pay stubs. Some refuse job offers so they can remain on unemployment.

But this is not the norm. The truth is that it is very difficult to qualify for aid. Our family just barely overqualified for food.

GRACE FOR THOSE WITH
AN INCOME PROBLEM

No doubt poverty in America is a complex issue. Even the definition of "poverty" is subjective, especially when compared to the state of the undeveloped world. But one thing we can all work on is changing our attitudes.

What if, instead of assuming the lady in front of you in the grocery store line is cheating the system, you imagined her husband has lost his job or has passed away and left her to care for their children on her own? What if, instead of judging the contents of the grocery carts of those with WIC checks—because God forbid they ever buy toys for their children or nail polish for themselves—you thank God that they somehow have the means for a few small wants in addition to their needs? Let's stop to consider that perhaps someone gave them a gift card, or maybe these are foster parents who are using government checks to feed the children in their care and are purchasing the extras in their carts with their own funds.

Let's all—me included—work to never make assumptions.

BUT IT DOESN'T SEEM FAIR!

It can be tempting to look at what welfare recipients receive as unfair. After all, families on food stamps can get hundreds of dollars of groceries free each month, WIC mothers and children get free food as well, and those on Medicaid obtain free healthcare. (It's not truly free, as tax dollars do pay for it all. This is when we must trust in Jesus' command, as I noted in the last chapter, to "give back to Caesar what is Caesar's and to God what is God's.") It can be especially hard to avoid becoming bitter about this when your income level just barely prevents you from receiving aid as well. This was the case with our family and food stamps. We were considered the working poor, yet we were not poor enough to get an EBT card, which would have provided upwards of $600 worth of groceries for our family each month.

Some people never pay back, and that's OK.

What I'm about to say may anger a few: It does no good to resent those who cannot pay back the government for the resources they have used. Yes, the goal is for those who use welfare to rise up, create more income, and pour into the system as much as and more than what they have used. This is what, praise God, our family has been able to accomplish. However, there will be some who will never have the resources to reciprocate. I love what Jesus says about the poor in Luke 14:13–14: "But when you give a banquet, invite the poor, the crippled, the lame, the blind, and you will be blessed. Although they cannot repay you, you will be repaid at the resurrection of the righteous."

Practicing gratitude for what we *do* have instead of looking at what others are getting for free can help us keep things in perspective. We can choose to become bitter about what we don't have and what others do (either through charity or government resources or more income), or we can choose to rise above our circumstances and seek to grow. Even while we used government resources, our family felt motivated to increase our income, once we realized we simply didn't earn enough money. Looking back, I'm so glad we didn't allow bitterness to take root.

HOW CAN THE CHURCH HELP?

If you are a North American Christian, the reality of our society's vast wealth presents you with an enormous responsibility, for throughout the Scriptures God's people are commanded to show compassion to the poor. In fact, doing so is simply part of our job description as followers of Jesus Christ (Matt. 25:31–46). While the biblical call to care for the poor transcends time and place, passages such as 1 John 3:17 should weigh particularly heavy on the minds and hearts of North American Christians: "If anyone has material possessions and sees his brother in need but has no pity on him, how can the love of God be in him?" Of course, there is no "one-size-fits-all" recipe

*for how each Christian should respond to this biblical
mandate. Some are called to pursue poverty alleviation
as a career, while others are called to do so as volunteers.
Some are called to engage in hands-on, relational ministry,
while others are better suited to support frontline workers
through financial donations, prayer, and other types of
support. Each Christian has a unique set of gifts, callings,
and responsibilities that influence the scope and manner
in which to fulfill the biblical mandate to help the poor.*

STEVE CORBETT AND BRIAN FIKKERT,
WHEN HELPING HURTS

We've established that poverty in America (and across the
world for that matter) is a problem that's here to stay, and that
believers sometimes struggle with casting judgment on those
who rely on government resources instead of the church to meet
their needs. But how *can* the church help alleviate some of the
pressures low-income earners face? Is there a way for the church
to breathe dignity into those living on welfare while also helping
them break free from financial crises?

I don't pretend to have the answers to this, but after walking the
path of low-income living ourselves for a season, I have some ideas:

Learn to work with *instead of* against *government programs.*

There are some government-funded organizations I will never
support, such as Planned Parenthood, but what if the church
joined with government programs that provide food and medical care?

As I stated in the previous chapter, a common argument I hear
from Christians who oppose government aid programs is that it is
the church's job to care for the poor, not the government's. When

I look at the biblical commands to care for the poor throughout the entirety of Scripture, I have to agree with this. However, what happens to the poor when the church as a whole is not doing its job?

We live in a culture that largely celebrates pouring millions of dollars into state-of-the-art church buildings while the church's low-income neighbors are hungry, thirsty, and in dire medical straits. Churches in America often operate out of budgets that place greater emphasis on personnel and member needs than on benevolence funds. It's not wrong to invest in discipleship and growth programs for believers; I'm thankful to be part of a church that prioritizes helping Christians mature while also giving to our neighbors in need. I'm also of the opinion that we need to pay our pastors well. But when meeting intellectual and spiritual needs within the church supersedes reaching out to the world in which Christ has called us—whether through time or money—something is off balance.

Yes, churches have many resources at their fingertips, but the government does as well. There are faith-based programs that are already working with government organizations and seeing great results. Across the country, there are nonprofit, federally-funded health centers that provide medical, dental, and pharmacy services to those living in poverty. Churches can and are partnering with these to serve others. As well, there are organizations like Act for Justice, a Dallas, Texas, faith-based nonprofit that helps educate people in crime-ridden neighborhoods about their rights to legal representation.

On an individual scale, believers can minister to the poor in more tangible ways by seeking employment with nonprofits funded by government grants. Before I got married, I worked for a charity called Latino Memphis that helped low-income Hispanic immigrants with a variety of issues. Because, as a Christian, I carry the Holy Spirit with me wherever I work, I was able to use my job as an opportunity to plant seeds of the gospel with both immigrants and my coworkers. Beyond employment, Christians can give to these faith and government partnerships by volunteering their time and donating money and supplies.

While the argument may stand that using government resources can limit a charity's ability to proclaim the gospel, I believe meeting the physical needs of suffering individuals can go a long way in opening the door to meeting their spiritual needs as well.

Join God where He is already at work.

> *We are not bringing Christ to poor communities. He has been active in these communities since the creation of the world, sustaining them, as Hebrews 1:3 says, by His powerful Word. Hence, a significant part of working in poor communities involves discovering and appreciating what God has been doing there for a LONG time.*
>
> STEVE CORBETT AND BRIAN FIKKERT,
> *WHEN HELPING HURTS*

We must remember that God is always working, with or without us. His work among the poor is not dependent upon us, but we can partner with Him to serve the poor.

Where are the poor? Low-income neighborhoods might be the obvious answer. You're guaranteed to find them at your local soup kitchen or homeless shelter as well as your local Department of Social Services. But having been low-income myself, I've learned to think outside the box.

For more than a decade, the trend has been to start churches among small groups gathered in coffee shops. While this idea appealed to me during my twenties, I now see how this location limits a church's ability to meet the very people it is called to care for. I love what Richard Beck, author of *The Slavery of Death*, had to say about churches creating spaces for building relationships with the poor:[1]

> The working poor don't hang out in coffee shops with their Mac laptops. Nor can they afford $4 specialty drinks. So a coffee shop isn't going to be frequented by the working poor—White, Black or Hispanic—in our neighborhood. To be sure, a cool coffee shop would attract White hipsters, but that's not the demographic of our church neighborhood. So what would be . . . a place that would serve the neighborhood but could also be a place where people would spend time talking and forming relationships?

Before reading Beck's words, I saw no wrong in the hip coffee-shop churches that have infiltrated Christian culture. I attended one during college, and I always lauded the ability of these church environments to appeal to people who might never enter a traditional church building. Even when we were living on a low income, I wouldn't have given a second thought to attending a coffee-shop church—albeit without an expensive Mac laptop and a specialty drink. Now I know that my upper-middle-class upbringing clouded my view of the types of churches that attract the poor. I initially began to grasp this when I was writing for newspapers and had the opportunity to interview individuals and families from all backgrounds and walks of life. There was a time when I wanted to invite some of them to my church, but

I stopped myself when I realized that it was hard for Will and me—two highly-educated but low-income individuals—to feel at home in our congregation. It would be even harder for those who were living at our income level but had no college degrees to fit in with parishioners in high-income jobs and with letters behind their names. Beck's ideal setting for a church among the poor is a laundromat:

> What middle and upper class people seriously take for granted is taking a few steps to throw a load of laundry into the washing machine. Can you imagine the hassle and the disruption to your day if you had to drive—or, more likely, walk or take a bus—to a laundromat? To say nothing of the lost time standing around attending your clothing as it washes and dries? And then there's the money to run the machines, money you might need for dinner . . . But . . . do you know what people do as they sit around waiting for their clothing to wash and dry? They talk. As neighbors . . . Laundromats meet a need in a way a caramel macchiato cannot. To say nothing of the blessing it would be to hand out free quarters or provide an attendant so that errands could be run while clothing was being cleaned or dried. Perfect ministry opportunities for church members wanting to serve and get to know neighbors.[2]

Educate!

Two kinds of education need to happen: (1) education of the poor and (2) education of the middle and upper classes to the world in which the low income live. I was blinded to the world of the have-nots until I became one. I didn't understand the privilege into which I had been born and how that played into Will and me being able to improve our financial situation.

Will and I both have college degrees. When we married, we had zero college debt (something I realize many of you reading are probably still battling). Why? We both had scholarships, and our parents also helped out. In fact, the only college expenses I ever had to cover were my books. Even though we were technically classified as the "working poor" because of our income level, I would soon learn how fortunate we were. We had parents who had warm homes and extra square footage if we needed to move in with them. No, it wouldn't have been ideal, but we never feared being homeless or destitute. We were making it, albeit just barely.

Realizing the privilege into which I had been born and raised was a game-changer. I was blind to it before we struggled. But then, for the first time, I realized many people don't have the same opportunities, even in the United States. Those born into poverty have an incredibly hard road ahead of them. Those born into a middle-or high-income family have a head start.

What is the solution? It's complicated, and I don't pretend to have it all figured out. But what I do know is that a little empathy and humility can go a long way in helping us realize that those who have fallen on hard times are not necessarily lazy or "taking advantage" of the system. Those of us who are born into financially stable homes have a leg up. Most of the time, there's nothing we've done to make this happen. And it's high time we admit that.

Because Will and I each received a good education, we knew of ways to increase our income (once we realized that was our problem). Seeking to provide a good education for others—especially those unable to afford private or post-secondary education without scholarships—can be one way in which we make strides forward to alleviate poverty and break the cycle of long-term welfare living. We can do this by advocating for public schools even if we choose other educational methods, such as homeschooling or private school, for our children. Instead of grumbling that our tax dollars are going to fund schools our children might never attend, why not donate school supplies or after-school snacks? A ministry my church supports, Food for Days, provides after-school snacks for impoverished public school children. For some of these children, the snacks are the only food they have to eat at home. We can seek to meet the needs of public school children whose parents might not be able to afford even the basics, much less pay to send them to private schools or quit their jobs to homeschool. Public schools are among the institutions that are training our future leaders, the adults our own adult children will live and work alongside day. Instead of lamenting the damage they do (as I've heard some people do), why not seek to improve them?

Build relationships.

The church today can talk about giving to the poor, but how often do we—me included—walk among them and look into their eyes, acknowledging that we are no better than they? Better off financially? Yes. But better people? Never.

Our time on government aid helped me see others for who they are—people just like me. People who have hopes and dreams and ambitions. People who have been born into or fallen on hard times. People who, for the most part, want a way out but don't know one exists. The conversations I had in the Department of Social Services with other government aid recipients burst my middle-income bubble and helped me see more clearly the humanity of the people who need government aid to get by.

A SHORT-TERM SOLUTION INSTEAD OF
A LONG-TERM LIFESTYLE (FOR MOST)

I believe government aid should be a short-term solution instead of a long-term lifestyle for most families. (The exception is for disabled individuals who are unable to work.) Yes, there were days when it felt like we would never overcome our financial frustrations and would always need to live on welfare. Still, we wanted to break out of the cycle because we value hard work and know that our government systems are not set up to support families for life. In chapter 13, we will dive deeper into how those with an income problem can make more money for their families.

I am a pull-myself-up-by-my-bootstraps type of gal, but I still remember feeling as if there was no light at the end of the tunnel for us. Many others feel the same. Some people's bootstraps are so long and tattered, and their hands so scarred or arthritic, that they have a hard time pulling them up all by themselves. They need someone to tie their shoes, hold their hands, and help them stumble along until they are walking. And then help them walk until they can run.

Everyone has a story to tell. Our time on welfare taught me that financial need can land on any of us—*any of us*—in an instant. It only takes one job loss, one unexpected pregnancy, one tragedy. This isn't about cop-outs. It's about compassion. It's about pulling our heads out of the sand and understanding that instead of choosing between gymnastics or dance classes, many people must choose between paying the electricity bill or buying groceries. Instead of choosing steak or chicken, they choose red beans or white.

Sometimes I feel as if I'm still standing with my feet in two worlds, and to be honest, I wouldn't have it any other way. I believe we walked *there* so God could use us *here*.

What will it take to turn prideful pity into a picture of grace? I am only one woman, but I'm calling for a paradigm shift. Our Christian culture tends to give most generously at Thanksgiving and Christmas. But people are hungry year-round. We donate old clothes to those "less fortunate," but do we ever look into their eyes? Try to understand their lives? See them as human?

Why does a compassionate Christian sound like an oxymoron to so much of the world when Scripture clearly calls for compassion? Why are we so often divided? Our compassion, friends, can lead people to the gospel. The God of hope—your God, my God—can change our attitudes. Can grip our hearts. Can evoke empathy for our neighbors.

"The King will reply, 'Truly I tell you, whatever you did for one of the least of these brothers and sisters of mine, you did for me.'" (Matthew 25:40)

THIRTEEN

CREATING MORE INCOME

Dishonest money dwindles away,
but whoever gathers money little by little makes it grow.

PROVERBS 13:11

WINTER 2009

I've always enjoyed weaving words together. Everything about writing thrills me—getting ideas onto paper to forming sentences and paragraphs, rewriting, polishing, and editing. I've never felt skilled at much else, but writing makes me come alive.

Soon after we moved back to North Carolina in 2009, I thought about Frank, my former editor at *The Salisbury Post*. I interned at the *Post* right after college, and Frank had offered me a full-time job. I chose to move to Costa Rica instead.

I hadn't written in six years. Plagued with depression and reverse culture shock after my stint in Costa Rica, I'd lost my inspiration. Even my journals sat empty, with only a few scribbles here and there. Motivated by the prospect of adding income to our family while working from home, I mustered the courage to send Frank an email. *What if he didn't remember me? What if he asked for writing samples? Would he be upset with me for not accepting his job offer all those years before and chasing a*

Latin American adventure instead? But, I figured, the worst he could say was "no."

> Dear Frank,
>
> I'm not sure if you remember me, but I interned for you at *The Salisbury Post* in the summer of 2003. It was one of the best jobs I've ever held. When I left the *Post*, I spent a year in Costa Rica, where I met my husband. We moved to the Memphis area, and I've spent the past five years working with Latino immigrants and teaching. Our family—including our one-year-old daughter—recently moved back to the area, and I'm interested in re-honing my writing skills. I was excited when I discovered you are now managing editor at the *Herald*, as we are living nearby. Are you accepting any freelancers? I would covet the opportunity if one exists.
>
> Sincerely,
> *Erin*

I was surprised but delighted when Frank wrote back. My heart danced with joy for the first time in weeks. Did God, perhaps, want me to write again?

> Dear Erin,
>
> I absolutely remember you. I offered you a permanent position at the *Post*, but you had your heart set on Costa Rica. I indeed have a position for a freelancer, and we're starting a new paper in your town. I would love to meet about this in person. Is there a day you can come by the office?
>
> *Frank*

I met with Frank the following week. We had a great conversation, and Frank offered me a full-time editing job, but my heart was at home with our daughter. It had been my dream to stay home with my children. Plus, the salary I would've earned as the editor of a small-town newspaper would have barely covered the cost of childcare. *Would Frank still take a freelancer?* I had to ask.

"I had a feeling you would turn this one down," Frank said, laughing. "But if I can hire you as a freelancer, I would be honored."

Finally, I was writing again.

$\sim$

I ended up writing hundreds of articles for Carolina Weekly newspapers. Eventually the job led to a blog that would provide a full-time income and to the agent who would land me a deal for the book you now hold in your hands. Even when we couldn't see it, God had a plan.

Another editor at the newspaper, Justin, was one of two individuals who gave me the idea to start blogging. I had no idea there was potential for income in blogging, much less a full-time income. When I became pregnant again, Justin asked if I wanted to deviate from regular feature writing and try composing a column, wherein I would chronicle the ups and downs of motherhood. To my surprise, I loved it. Column writing and blog writing were similar, Justin said. I might have a knack for it as well.

It was around that time that my college roommate Brantley suggested the same thing. "You know, some bloggers make an income for their families," she said. "You should try it."

If you feel stuck with an income problem, I have good news. With hard work and imagination, you can improve your financial situation. In this chapter, I hope to inspire you to think outside the box. We'll explore a number of different ways you can create more income by discovering your unique personality, passions, and purpose as well as your skills and talents.

CHANGE CAREERS OR JUST KEEP ON TRUCKIN'?

When Randy told us we had an income problem—even with my writing for the newspaper and Will working extra jobs at his school—we weren't sure which way to turn. Should we start our own business? Should I go back to work full time? Should Will consider a career change?

It took some trial and error and plenty of prayer before we knew the path God had for us. His plan is different for everyone; I encourage you to not shut any doors before exploring all options.

At first, we looked into Will changing careers. He had been teaching for more than a decade, but there's little room for financial growth in education. If we wanted to support our family without the help of government aid, teaching wouldn't work long-term—at least not in our state.

But Will's attempts to switch careers turned cold. He sent applications to various companies, and we never heard back from most of them. We were living in the midst of a recession, and unemployment was at a high. At least Will *had* a job; in his search for one that paid more, he was competing against thousands. When I discovered that an acquaintance's husband had successfully transitioned from education to the corporate world, it felt like divine opportunity. The couple met us for dinner, and we talked about how Will could realistically change careers. The man even set up an appointment for Will at his company, but the supervisor discouraged Will. He walked away feeling defeated.

Our hopes deflated, but we now realize the corporate world was not God's path for Will or our family. He had plans to provide for us through the entrepreneurial and writing world in a way that synergized our individual skill sets.

If your first attempt at creating more income for your family falls flat, don't despair. Like *The Little Engine That Could*, try, try, and try again. You never know what opportunities lie right around the corner. Becoming entrepreneurs has brought us incredible opportunities that we would have missed if Will had gotten a job in corporate America. What was upsetting at the time turned out to be a blessing in disguise.

THE LIFE OF A WORKING MOM

Later in this chapter, we will discuss entrepreneurship in more depth. But if you're *desperate* for money, this isn't the time to take out a credit line and invest in a business that may or may not result in the income of your dreams. It's the time to get a waitressing job on the side, to work for someone else (instead of starting your own business), to go back to work in any capacity. In today's society, working moms—whether they work full-time or part-time or work from home—are the norm. In my next book, I'll share how you can be a stay-at-home mom even if your husband isn't bringing in six figures. But the truth is, some families' financial frustrations are in such dire need of an increased income that mom might have to go to work full-time, at least temporarily.

When I was pregnant with our first child, Will and I planned for me to stay home with her. But the unforeseen economic crash forced me to go back to work when she was only six weeks old. My job provided our health insurance; we couldn't survive without it.

I'll never forget leaving my six-week-old baby in her swing the morning I went back to work. My friend Lexie came to our house to babysit. Saying goodbye to my sweet infant broke my heart. I worked full-time until she was six months old. I don't look back with regret, though; instead, I think about all God taught me and about how He provided for our family.

Are you a working mom who would rather stay home? Or are you a stay-at-home mom drowning in debt or a low income who might need to go back to work? Either way, you are not alone, and God has a plan for your life and for the lives of your children. If you must work full time outside the home, know that it can be temporary. An uprising of work-at-home moms has swept our culture for the past decade, and there are many more options at your fingertips (or computer keyboard!) today than there were for our parents' generation.

DON'T COMPROMISE YOUR VALUES FOR A QUICK BUCK

While I was moonlighting as a freelance writer, Will was working several extra jobs of his own. His school needed a Saturday school teacher and after-school teacher. Will accepted both positions. He also taught summer school. Eventually his principal offered him the opportunity to teach an extra class during his planning period. None of these additional jobs paid much, but every little bit counted.

When you're in a financially desperate position, it can be tempting to accept every money-making offer. I urge you to exercise caution and consider all options before committing to a gig that might compromise your values. An example of this was when Will's principal approached him about teaching an "abstinence education" class after school. I'll never forget the day Will told me about this new opportunity. The curriculum came with pre-written lesson plans, and the job would entail only a few extra hours of teaching per week. He would earn an additional several thousand dollars a year! The position sounded like a perfect fit. It required less time than other options we were exploring, paid more money, and was in the same location as his current job. It felt like an answer to our prayers.

However, after attending training for the class, Will came home frustrated.

"What's wrong?" I asked. "Did the orientation not go like you imagined?"

"It's misleading to call it 'abstinence education,'" Will said. "It's really a sex ed class."

In the end, it wasn't worth compromising our morals. Within a few months, however, we saw our situation turn around as God began to provide for our needs in a different way, honoring Will's commitment to our values. To our surprise, the hobby blog I started on a whim started bringing in more and more money each month. Soon it would become our primary source of income.

SIDE JOBS THAT TURN INTO SOMETHING MORE

When we were trying to determine the best way for us to create more income, I made a list of different business ideas. I was willing to try anything, so I didn't focus on my skills and passions as much as what I saw others doing. My list was long and unrealistic. How could I expect to make money as a gluten-free baker when I don't particularly enjoy baking, and how could I become a seamstress if I fumbled to simply thread my sewing machine? I laugh when I look back at everything we tried, and I'm thankful for how every little bit added up—for how God met and continues to meet our needs. It's important to note that not every job or home-based business opportunity is ideal for everyone. Knowing your unique personality, passions, and purpose as well as your skill set and natural talents can help determine if a business venture is a good fit for you or your spouse. We will address personality and purpose, specifically, later in this chapter.

The following section will help you explore a variety of ways to begin creating more income for your family, hopefully sparking inspiration as you seek to do just that.

Virtual assistant

A virtual assistant (VA) is a remote administrative assistant, usually on contract. As long as you have a computer, internet access, and a phone, you don't need to leave home! VAs can work for individuals in other towns, other states, or even in other countries.

One of my first attempts at creating more income for our family was as a VA for a blogger. I quickly discovered that I'm *not* cut out for VA work. While being a VA is the perfect job for some, it wasn't the job for me. I'm simply not organized enough! Years later, I'm thrilled to have given several VAs jobs through my business. If VA work interests you, check out the ebook *The Bootstrap VA* by Lisa Morosky. Although Lisa has seen her VA business pave the way for financial success and generous giving for her family, she sees the true value of her business in relationships:

"I'm able to be a stay-at-home mom," she said. "I get to use my skills to benefit businesses and people who are doing great work. I've been able to help other women start their own virtual assistant businesses. What started as a way to earn some extra money and new skills turned into my own God-given ministry."

Freelance editor

Another job I tried was freelance editing. This type of work married my interests and educational background since I enjoy any work related to language arts, and my bachelor's degree is in journalism with a minor in English. We live in an era where editing opportunities abound. I mostly edited ebooks, but I also worked as the content editor for a contributor-based blog. Although I thrived at editing and enjoyed it for several years, I didn't charge enough to make it something that could turn into a realistic, long-term income for our family. Plus, I longed to create stories of my own.

One of my friends, Dawn Mena of GetCaptivatingCopy.com, provides freelance editing as part of her business model.

"It's a great way to supplement my income, while doing something positive that helps others share their stories with confidence," she said.

If you're interested in freelance editing, I recommend emailing your favorite bloggers with a job pitch or checking job postings on sites like upwork.com, an online platform where freelancers can connect with businesses to find home-based work.

Social media manager

After our second daughter was born, I started using cloth diapers. My favorite online store was a small start-up called Jack Be Natural. After building a relationship with the store owners through their Facebook page, they asked if I would be interested in *managing* the page. Not only did I get a discount on diapers, but they also paid me an hourly wage.

Because I'm naturally relational, running their Facebook page was a breeze. I worked as the social media manager at Jack Be Natural for about a year, until my blog grew to the point that I needed to focus on it full time.

If you think you have the personality to be a social media manager, I encourage you to take the initiative and contact some of your favorite small business owners. Several ladies have helped run my social media at thehumbledhomemaker.com for years now, and there isn't a business owner I know who wouldn't mind extra support in this department.

Making and selling

I'm not crafty, nor am I good with my hands. I'm not sure what I was thinking when I told Will I wanted to learn how to sew and create products to sell. But he believed in me, so he sold his Xbox and purchased a secondhand embroidery machine. I made one baby quilt before realizing sewing is *not* my forte. Making and selling crafty items isn't my skill set or my passion.

However, many a mom has generated income for her family by selling homemade items at places like Etsy, Hyena Cart, local craft shows, and even via a personal website.

My friend Lexie gained an interest in natural skincare products when her children were babies. She began making non-toxic deodorant, lip balm, and lotion for her family. Friends soon offered to pay her to make products for them as well. Within a few years, Lexie's hobby had turned into Lexie:Naturals, a business with hundreds of customers around the country.

Direct sales or multi-level marketing

Selling makeup through a direct sales company was my first dip into the ocean of entrepreneurial living. I tried this when we were newlyweds. I was teaching full time, but I thought direct sales might provide supplemental income for us. I was wrong. Because I'm *not* a natural salesperson, instead of making money, I ended up spending it in order to meet my required monthly sales quotas!

Direct sales wasn't a match for *me*, but it can be an incredibly fruitful income source. Chris and Andrea, friends of Will's from college, took a risk using their 2015 tax refund to invest in starting a LuLaRoe business. It's paid off. LuLaRoe sells trendy leggings, tops, skirts, and dresses for women and little girls. The company has exploded in popularity, and the couple bought into it at just the right time. After several years of financial frustration, Chris and Andrea are seeing LuLaRoe help them go from barely surviving to more than just making it financially. "All our bills are paid, we no longer need food assistance, and we've just returned from our first vacation as a family of three," Andrea told me in 2016. "It's changed our lives in so many more ways than I can list."

With hundreds of direct sales companies in operation, it can be overwhelming to decide which one to join. Choose a company with products you are so passionate about that you would share them with others even if you didn't get paid. My friend Bethany, a long-time health enthusiast and mom of many, credits the success she's seen with the natural supplements company Plexus to the fact that the company merges her passions for wellness and business. Being a Plexus ambassador has given her family a second income and increased freedom, but "the best part is the products are products we believe in," she said. "They've been a benefit to our health as well as to the health of friends and family."

Graphic design and art skills

Will has enjoyed graphic design since his college days, and when we were newlyweds, he made custom cards for family and friends. When we were seeking to create more income, he began selling his designs. It was fun to watch God provide through this side job. One time, someone paid him double because they thought Will wasn't charging enough. This happened at the same time we needed a new bed for one of our little girls, and the extra money paid for it.

If you have graphic design skills, check out freelance sites like Upwork or Fiverr. Or try selling designs on Etsy. Bloggers and small business owners pay freelance designers to create graphics like invitations, event posters, printables, ebook covers, and more. It never hurts to approach a business owner and offer your services.

In the same vein, those gifted with other talents such as painting, pottery, and ceramics might want to consider how those can become business ventures. When she discovered she had a knack for the art of face painting, Illinois mom Joy created The Joy of Face Painting, sharing her talents at children's birthday parties and other events.

Freelance photography

When I worked as a freelance writer, Will often joined me on assignment as a photographer. This was a win-win because he got paid for every published photo, and the newspaper didn't have to send out a staff photographer with me on assignment. Others with photography talents have created their own portrait or lifestyle photography businesses.

A Note on Advertising Your Freelance Work

When it comes to advertising your freelancing, I've found that word of mouth works wonders when you're first starting. Volunteering your skills for free or at a discounted rate to two or three clients in exchange for reviews and referrals will gain you great returns and more income later. But perhaps the strongest advantage our generation has when it comes to building businesses is the power of the internet. You can advertise for free on sites like Craigslist, and once you have a little money to invest, try non-traditional forms of advertising like Facebook ads or promoted pins on Pinterest. Beth Anne Schwamberger, creator of the popular Brilliant Business Moms network, has produced e-courses that teach people how to harness the potential of both of these. For more information, visit her website, brilliantbusinessmoms.com.

Tutoring and teaching classes

When we were seeking to make extra money, both Will and I tutored students. Tutoring—whether online or in person—is a good option for teachers or experts in certain subjects. Will also sold teaching tools through teacherspayteachers.com. This online marketplace allows teachers to buy and sell lesson plans, worksheets, and other activities.

In addition to tutoring at a local elementary school when our firstborn was a baby, I taught Spanish to a homeschool family's children. Consider if your knowledge or expertise is something others—children or adults—would be interested in learning. Teaching others to play musical instruments, create art, speak a foreign language, or learn computer skills all come to mind as possibilities. You can tutor one-on-one or in live workshops.

Creating online courses

Another venture you can try is creating an online course that meets a felt need. Web-based classes have surged in popularity over the past few years. Many of my blogging colleagues earn a full-time income through their online courses. From cooking courses to classes on health and wellness and even by creating online fitness studios, moms are using their skill sets to educate others while earning an income from home. Teachable, Thinkific, and Course Cats are three online course platforms. My mentor Holly and I used Course Cats to create our What's 4 Dinner Challenge meal planning course.

Buying and reselling secondhand items

As I mentioned in chapter 8, my grandmother embraced her entrepreneurial spirit out of a personal passion and necessity when she became a single mom. She spent her weekdays frequenting thrift stores and her weekends shopping yard sales to purchase inventory for her business. A lover of fine antiques and secondhand shopping, Granny turned her skills into a business that supported her for the rest of her life. Many families today have created extra income by buying and reselling secondhand items—clothing, toys, shoes, baby gear, furniture, home decor, and more—via eBay, Amazon, online yard sales, consignment shops, Craigslist, and OfferUp.

Open your own bed and breakfast

The rise in home sharing has made renting out an extra room through a service like AirBnB or VRBO a viable income option.

Our friends Jacqueline and Jack purchased a home with enough extra space to create several AirBnB rooms. Less than a year into this business, renting out parts of their home has proven successful, and there is potential for the couple to pay off their entire mortgage through the investment. "Having a gift for hospitality and enjoying hosting, we felt this would be an ideal venture for us," Jack said. "Not only have we been given the opportunity to have our mortgage paid for, but we have been able to meet guests from dozens of different countries. We love the fact that, by staying with us, they are able to see a glimpse of Christ."

WHEN IN DOUBT, LEARN YOUR PERSONALITY

I recommend that everyone take at least one personality test to help them discover the type of work for which they're best wired. Three personality tests I endorse include the Myers-Briggs Type Indicator (MBTI), the Enneagram, and the Four Temperaments Test.

The MBTI focuses on an individual's strengths and uses four indexes to categorize people into one of sixteen personality types. The Enneagram classifies people into one of nine interconnected personality types and helps determine how they behave when they are at their healthiest as well as when they're in an unhealthy state. The Four Temperaments Test rates whether a person is one of four temperaments—a sanguine (optimistic and social), choleric (short-tempered or irritable), melancholic (analytical and quiet), or phlegmatic (relaxed and peaceful).

These assessments can help you discover the best type of work for you. For example, a sanguine like me loves working with people, but I'm not as great with analytical-type jobs as a melancholic would be. You can find free versions of all three personality tests online.

BE CLEAR IN YOUR PURPOSE

Too often we assume that God has increased our income to increase our standard of living, when his stated purpose is to increase our standard of giving.

RANDY ALCORN, *MONEY, POSSESSIONS, AND ETERNITY*

Your purpose is to make more money, right? But what is your purpose *behind* making more money? Do you want to increase your standard of living? Do you want to be able to afford extracurricular activities for your children? Do you want to meet certain financial goals, like paying off debt or your mortgage, funding college or retirement, or buying a new car? Or do you already make enough money to live and you've met your financial goals, but you desire to give more freely to others?

Knowing your purpose in creating more income helps you stay focused. For example, if your goal is to make some fun money to satisfy your craving for gourmet coffee, then a side job that brings in a *little* extra will do the trick. But if you're living at or below poverty level, you'll need to think more creatively about how to generate a longer-term, viable income for your family.

Before we met with Randy, Will and I were spinning our wheels with at least six extra income streams. None of these added up to the income we needed to support our family. The odd jobs we took on helped, but we had to focus on long-term options before we saw our situation improve. Working so many different jobs at once hindered our family time. When Will was working both after school and Saturday school, the girls and I felt like we never saw him. On top of that, I would stay up all hours of the night writing newspaper articles and working on my blog.

This took a toll on my energy level the next day, which made for a grumpy mama more often than I care to admit.

My side job eventually turned into our primary income and became the business Will and I now run together. It blends both of our gifts perfectly—my flair for writing, editing, marketing, and connecting with people combined with Will's knack for photography, graphic design, and administration.

DON'T EXPECT YOUR DREAM JOB TO HAPPEN OVERNIGHT

While we're now able to provide for our family through something we're both passionate about, it clearly wasn't always the case. As I've recounted, Will and I worked odd jobs for *years*—often outside of our personalities, passions, skills, and talents. It's paid off, and we've seen God's hand throughout the process, but it was tiring at times. My friend Kelly, a mother of four, says it hasn't been easy watching her husband work so many extra jobs, but it's been worth it. "My husband has three jobs—at Chick-Fil-A, as the media pastor at our church, and self-employed with a music teaching ministry. This year we've been able to start a savings account and pay off about $4,000 in debt. It's incredible to see this happening. We still have debt, but we're realizing it doesn't control us!"

TREAT YOUR INCOME GENERATORS AS REAL BUSINESSES BECAUSE THEY *ARE*

It's important to treat your income generators like real businesses. When I first started blogging, we made the mistake of not keeping good records of the money I was earning, and we didn't separate our personal bank account from business funds. We had no idea that pocket change would one day turn into a full-time income.

Thankfully, even when we were working odd jobs, we knew we needed help with our taxes. We started with a bookkeeper. That worked out fine until the year we made more money than we had anticipated. Right before we purchased our home, we asked the bookkeeper to give us an estimate on how much we would owe in taxes that year. We wanted to leave enough reserves in our savings account to pay both Uncle Sam *and* put a decent amount of money toward a down payment on our house. She told us the figure, and we felt free to put down a sizable chunk of cash.

But two weeks after we purchased our home, the bookkeeper called me with grim news:

"Erin, I underestimated your tax payment . . . by half."

We went into panic mode, upset about the miscalculation but thankful we had months to gather funds to pay our bill.

We earned enough to pay the full amount by April 15, but we learned our lesson. Our business needed a certified public accountant (CPA). A CPA can keep your books, prepare your taxes, and help you make decisions for your business, like whether you should file as an LLC or S corp. Hiring a CPA has been one of the best investments we've made in the life of our business.

Also, consider joining business support groups. Check out your local Chamber of Commerce or online resources like Brilliant Business Moms and iBloom, both networks for Christian women in business. Consider attending a professional conference like Business Boutique, which is perfect for female entrepreneurs.

UNEXPECTED GIFTS FROM YOUR SIDE GIG

Beyond creating an income source for our family, God used writing to heal my heart during a challenging season. I was overwhelmed as a wife, mother, and homemaker, and we were in a hopeless period of financial anxiety. When I wrote heartwarming feature stories of triumph over tragedy for the newspapers, I channeled my pain into the stories of others. I saw their victories, and it gave me courage to face my own trials.

While in college, I had felt God moving me to write, and, really, He had been leading me in that direction since childhood. Years passed before that calling would become a reality. I ran from it for a long time. Only when we were desperate for money did I turn back to what God had been stirring in my heart from the time I learned to turn letters into words and words into sentences and sentences into paragraphs. Our time of hopelessness transformed into the vocation God had planned for me all along.

What is it for you, dear reader? How has God gifted you in a way that can bring your family out of a place of financial hardship while also bringing Him glory? How is He speaking to *your* heart right now?

FOURTEEN

REDEFINING THE AMERICAN DREAM

*We live in a society that breeds discontent by defining
success as bigger homes, nicer cars, and fuller closets.
Gratitude is the cure.*

JOSHUA BECKER, BECOMINGMINIMALIST.COM

SPRING 2011

I pulled up to the house where I was picking up a co-op order.
I had joined the food cooperative thinking it would help us
save money on healthy groceries. (It turned out it was still too
expensive; I only ordered once.) The home was in an affluent
neighborhood and had at least four bedrooms and a two-car
garage. A well-manicured lawn welcomed visitors, and an elegant
wreath graced the front door. I parked my mother's minivan in
the driveway and paused for a moment. *If only we had a house
like this. If only we had all that extra room and lived in a nice
neighborhood. If only we had more.*

These thoughts lasted only a few minutes before I shook them
off in order to get on with my day. I picked up my grocery order

and went on my way, wondering if she realized how differently the two of us lived. I drove around her neighborhood for a few minutes, admiring the spacious homes. I wondered if we would ever have a typical American home in the suburbs. *Lord, a house like one of these would be such a blessing*, I prayed silently. *It would be ideal to live in a 2,000-square-foot home in the suburbs—to own a house that could better hold our growing family and allow us to live the American Dream.*

That prayer made me recall how, years before, I had written in my journal, "My worst nightmare is to settle in the suburbs and simply embrace the American Dream. I want to live a life of purpose, and I don't want to just settle."

Now I was wishing for exactly that.

Once again, God brought to memory my childhood dream of serving internationally as a missionary. I'd wanted to do something radical—to live among the poor. Now I was living as a "poor person" in my own country (although we were still *incredibly* rich compared to most of the world). Had I really become so distanced from my childhood dream that I now wished for what was once my worst nightmare? I asked the Lord to make Jeremiah 2:2 a reality in my life: "I remember the devotion of your youth, how as a bride you loved me and followed."

WHAT IS THE AMERICAN DREAM, ANYWAY?

For decades the concept of the American Dream has embodied the freedom, prosperity, and success Americans can supposedly achieve through hard work. The essence of the dream is that the United States is a land of opportunity with few to no barriers for anyone who wants to achieve their dreams.[1]

While I admire the original intent of the American Dream, I wonder what our forefathers would think of what it's become.

IS THE AMERICAN DREAM A REALITY?

Those who use the American Dream as a basis for their value system have done so with the belief that every new generation of Americans can make more money than the generation before them. That assumption has proven true for decades. However, some economists predict that millennials will be the first generation of Americans who won't be financially better off than their parents.[2]

The financial landscape since the recession has changed economic morale. Millennials are expected to have a steeper climb up the ladder of success.[3] Whereas our parents and grandparents had many opportunities to achieve anything they set their minds to, those of us who came of age during the recession witnessed a crash that rivaled that of the Great Depression. Our parents and grandparents told us to work hard and get our college degrees, that those two things would ensure financial stability. Instead, we faced massive student loans, consumer debt, and a nationwide housing crisis that sent us into a financial tailspin as soon as we entered adulthood.

Many people believe that millennials were raised with a mentality of entitlement and the expectation that they would achieve the American Dream instantly upon entering adulthood. While many millennials have continued to live with their parents well into adulthood,[4] when they do leave the nest, some expect to immediately achieve the same socioeconomic status their parents took decades to achieve.

Will and I watched this cultural phenomenon happening

among our friends and experienced it ourselves. Why *can't* we start out in a 3,500 square foot home? Why *can't* we furnish our homes with new couches and recliners? Why *can't* we cook in kitchens with granite countertops while we're still in our twenties and thirties? We had to pause to consider that our parents took decades to acquire new furnishings, remodeled kitchens, and larger-than-average homes. But instead of waiting and working hard, many in our generation and the next have chosen to rack up credit card debt and live with massive mortgages to maintain the façade of living the American Dream.

While belief in the American Dream lasted for generations, some sociologists are now suggesting that those who have been able to achieve it have done so with the inherent advantage of being born into affluence. We should pause before accusing those who come from generations of low-income earners of being lazy as opposed to the "hardworking" middle and upper classes. Although Will and I lived on a low income for an incredibly challenging season, we had a leg up from the start. Although only one of our four parents has a college degree, they all worked hard to make sure we both earned degrees ourselves. Even at our lowest income level, we both had credentials that helped us find work and housing.

The truth of the matter is that upward mobility is more difficult for some than it is for others. Can the American Dream be achieved? Yes. Can everyone who works hard achieve it? No. Lack of education, post-recession economic instability, and even race can prevent people from achieving the American Dream.[5]

In his book *Days of Destruction, Days of Revolt*, author Chris Hedges wrote, "The vaunted American Dream, the idea that life will get better, that progress is inevitable if we obey the rules and work hard, that material prosperity is assured, has been replaced by a hard and bitter truth. The American Dream, we now know, is a lie."[6]

KEEPING UP WITH THE JONESES

As the definition of the American Dream has moved from the belief that hard work equals economic stability toward a sense of entitlement, the worldview has shifted to a mindset of "keeping up with the Joneses." This idiom can be traced back to a comic strip by the same name, circa 1913.[7] It refers to comparing your material possessions with those of your neighbor as a way to measure your social standing. The phrase gained momentum in Western societies in the mid-1970s, and material wealth as a measure of one's worth has been an overwhelming force ever since.[8] No longer are we content with hard work resulting in our needs and a few wants being met. Our society as a whole operates with an insatiable thirst for more.

For those of us who grew up in the '80s and '90s, keeping up with the Joneses wasn't a value system we *learned*. It was so ingrained in our culture that it was the default. My coworker lives in a large home? I should too. My classmate wears designer shoes? I should too. The family across the street takes a trip to Walt Disney World every summer? We should too. From homes to cars to clothing to vacations and everything else under the sun, the concept of the American Dream has morphed into the practice of keeping up with those around us. Instead of operating out of our own convictions to achieve personal goals and individual callings, we've depleted our savings accounts, dug ourselves into debt, and burdened our emotional and mental capacities with the stress that comes with keeping up with the Joneses. If only we realized the freedom of living within our means and practicing contentment.

A NEW MINDSET

I have learned to be content whatever the circumstances.

PHILIPPIANS 4:11

As disillusionment with the American Dream has risen, today's generation has begun to embrace a more minimalistic lifestyle, putting away aspirations of keeping up with the Joneses.

Author Rachel Jonat wrote about the keeping up with the Joneses mindset she grew up with in her book *The Minimalist Mom's Guide to Baby's First Year:*[9]

"Rich people once fascinated me," she wrote. "I grew up without a lot, but in a very wealthy community. Everyone always had more than we did. My schoolmates had newer clothes and bigger and nicer homes. I wanted that—not only for the status but also for the security. I wanted the security that I thought money brought."[10]

But Rachel and her family saw themselves make a paradigm shift after accumulating $82,000 in debt. They embraced a more minimalistic life and paid off $50,000 within a year.

"Money doesn't bring security. I know that now," Rachel wrote. "I know that a lot of my classmates lived in million dollar homes but had parents that couldn't sleep at night thinking about how much money they owed. I know that if I want security, the kind of security that I used to think came from having a lot of money, it will come not from a lot of money but from being free of debt and living a simple lifestyle. I know money doesn't bring happiness. But lowering your cost of living, paying down debt, and selling things you don't use can allow you to work less and live with less stress."[11]

Rachel's family worked hard to pay off their debts by committing to a countercultural lifestyle, resulting in less stress and a happiness they found material possessions couldn't bring.

"We still ate out occasionally, went on vacation, and continued to lead our lives," Rachel wrote. "Just with a lot less stuff."

Not only are those who are embracing a simpler lifestyle seeing renewed contentment in their lives, but they're also finding that by living with less, they can give more. Crystal Paine, aforementioned author and blogger behind MoneySavingMom .com, is on a mission to teach women that when they conquer financial frustration, they are free to give without hesitation.

"It's not about saving money so we can continuously upgrade our lifestyle and always be buying bigger and better things," Crystal said in her "31 Days of Giving on a Budget" series on MoneySavingMom.com.[12] "We want to live beneath our means so that we are able to give generously to others."

Despite owning a flourishing business, Crystal is convinced that money alone will never satisfy. "Money doesn't buy happiness," she wrote in her book *Money Making Mom*. "Money doesn't equal fulfillment. Money doesn't solve your emotional problems. Money doesn't give you purpose. If it did, the richest people in this world would be some of the happiest, most emotionally healthy people in existence. In reality, many of them are struggling through divorce, depression, and addictions, just like many people who don't make a seven-figure annual salary."[13]

A NEW AMERICAN DREAM

The bright economic landscape of yesterday's generation has dimmed, and the dreams we were told we could attain now seem like a mirage.

What if our generation could live with less than the Joneses while reaching for a new American Dream that leaves us fulfilled, less stressed, and reimagining "the good life"? What if we learned to be satisfied with our needs being met? What if we aligned our wants with God's design and our own callings, instead of basing them on what the family next door has chosen?

For generations, home ownership has been a hallmark of the American Dream. What if we *can* own homes without biting off more than we can afford? In the following section, we'll explore home ownership and discuss whether you should rent or buy. Then, we'll briefly look at how to purchase a vehicle with cash. If we can do it, you can too!

HOUSING

Overwhelmed by debt, and with the aftermath of the recession still fresh in their minds, many millennials feel it's too risky to sink their savings into a mortgage[14] (or they simply have no savings at all).

When Will and I were newlyweds in 2006—before the economic downturn—it wasn't uncommon for our young married friends to own a 1,500 to 2,000 square-foot home. We knew we couldn't afford much, but when our landlord decided to sell our rental, we decided to buy it. Will had quit his full-time job to go back to school, and even though he was making nearly as much as I was at his part-time job, we thought we were being smart by only using my teacher salary to qualify us for a loan. Our mortgage payment was around $700 a month after we applied the small down payment my parents had given us. This was slightly cheaper than what we had been paying in rent, so we never doubted we were making a wise financial choice by purchasing a home. What we didn't consider was how long we would be living in the area, whether the home would have good resale value in the future, and the extra expenses involved in home ownership. We especially didn't foresee a wide-scale economic crash. We ended up putting the house up for sale in 2008, less than a year after the recession began. It sat on the market for four years.

Future plans

We now know it's best to plan on living in a house for at least five years if you hope to turn a profit on it. When we purchased ours, we were unsure of our future plans. That should have been a red flag. Renting might seem like you're throwing away money, but unless you're confident you'll be living somewhere for at least half a decade, it might be your best option.

Resale value

When we purchased our home, the real estate market was hot. There had never been a precedent for the housing crisis that would occur just a year later. Even without the crash, though, our home wasn't a good prospect for resale. We had no hesitations about buying a two-bedroom home with no garage because we simply didn't realize that layout would be a hard sell down the road. Even a small home with three bedrooms and a garage will open up the market to families. Two-bedroom homes are usually limited to young couples, singles, or retired people wanting to downsize. Neighbors with homes the same square footage as ours but with a third bedroom and/or a garage had a much easier time finding buyers. Small homes in neighborhoods with larger homes are also easier to sell than the largest home in a neighborhood with smaller homes. We had this scenario going for us, but it was only one positive among many negatives.

The fine print

It's important to read the fine print on your mortgage and loan documents. It's also helpful to have an attorney go over these with you so that you understand everything involved in your agreement. We had no idea that our loan forbade us from renting out our home until it came time for us to sell it. Because we had rented it out off and on for four years, the bank considered it a real estate investment, which was against the terms of our loan. Even though we never made money on the home and only rented it out to cover the mortgage, it was still a breach of our contract. As a result, we weren't able to short sell the house (a step up from foreclosure).

Expenses of home ownership

There were also extra expenses we didn't consider: insurance (including PMI), repairs, and taxes should all be factored into your decision whether to buy or rent. When we had a low income, we couldn't afford basic home improvements, even with a low mortgage. Knowing our landlord was responsible for fixing anything that broke in our townhouse was a relief. Once, when the refrigerator stopped working, he even gave us a check to cover the cost of spoiled food.

The most expensive repairs a homeowner can face include replacing a roof, replacing the heating/cooling (HVAC) system, and replacing the hot water heater (in that order). It's important to inquire about the age of all three of these when purchasing a home. A new roof costs between $4,600 and $10,000 depending on the size of the roof, location of the home, and whether or not the homeowner uses a professional installation service or tries to do it himself. Shingle roofs last between fifteen and twenty-five years.

After we made an offer on our current home, the inspector came back with bad news: the roof only had two to three years left on it. We knew we wouldn't be able to afford a new roof in the near future, so we almost walked away from the contract.

We weren't trying to be demanding; rather, we knew we couldn't afford to replace the roof and didn't want to find ourselves in a precarious financial situation again. The sellers agreed to provide a new roof, and we took care of other, smaller repairs ourselves. The house also had the original HVAC and water heater, but we felt more confident proceeding with the contract knowing the most expensive repair was taken care of and would last another decade or two. After we had been in our house for three years, the original HVAC stopped working. Because we'd known we would have to replace it within a few years, we had saved the money to pay for a new one. It cost us around $4,000, but we didn't go into panic mode because we were prepared. The water heater will probably need to be replaced next, and our emergency fund should cover that cost.

A WORD ON PURCHASING VEHICLES

We didn't own a vehicle when we moved to North Carolina. It took us two years to purchase my parents' old (but reliable) minivan. We paid them with every newspaper check I earned. The freedom we felt when we made that final payment was exhilarating, and we set a goal to buy our next vehicle in cash. It seemed an insurmountable dream at the time, but we were able to do just that in 2014. Then, in 2016, we bought a second vehicle in cash. Here is how we did it:

We didn't shy away from driving an older, used vehicle.

We drove an older minivan for years, even as we watched friends driving around newer, nicer vehicles. When someone rear-ended me, our insurance company totaled the minivan. However, the defects were purely cosmetic; the engine still ran fine. We negotiated for them to allow us to keep the van and pay us a lesser amount of money in lieu of hauling it away. That van got us from point A to point B for two more years!

We lived below our means and saved our money.

When our income started increasing, we chose to continue living mostly on Will's salary. This meant we lived more frugally, but it allowed us to save cash to purchase these vehicles.

We avoided brand-new, pricier models.

Brand-new cars lose their value as soon as you drive them off the lot; we stuck to no-frills vehicles that were newer but not *new*.

We shopped around.

Will and my dad drove several hours to a neighboring state to check out vehicles, and we ended up buying a former rental car. This gave us the best bang for our buck!

The bottom line when it comes to car shopping is to forego trying to keep up with the Joneses. Don't deny yourself the freedom of *not* having a car payment!

HOPE FOR THE BEST, PLAN FOR THE WORST

Before we wrap up this chapter, I want to issue a caveat: We all have unique lives and situations. There will be times when you have to make choices that are better for you *at the moment*—even if they aren't necessarily the best possible choices overall. You might not be able to purchase a car in cash or put enough down on a home to avoid PMI—now. But choosing to live within your means instead of keeping up with the Joneses can get you there one day.

FIFTEEN

BANKRUPTCY OF THE HEART

How do you know if you are seeking Jesus for the right reasons? When He strips away everything that matters to you the most, does your faith increase or crumble? Jesus wants you to follow Him when things don't make sense. He gives and takes away. Blessed be His name.

BOBBY CONWAY, PASTOR OF LIFE
FELLOWSHIP CHARLOTTE AND AUTHOR
OF *DOUBTING TOWARD FAITH*

DECEMBER 23, 2011

I woke up abruptly to Will shaking me. I am normally a night owl, but first trimester fatigue had kicked in at just six weeks. I had fallen into a deep sleep around 9:00 p.m., and it was now 11:00. It was two days before Christmas, and I had dropped into bed without even putting on my pajamas. I was exhausted from mothering a toddler and baby, exhausted from pregnancy, and exhausted from staying up late and getting up early to try to make ends meet. I was exhausted from life.

"Erin! Wake up!" Will whispered urgently, not wanting to wake the girls. "It's Randy! He's had a heart attack!"

I rubbed my eyes and asked, "Randy who?"

I tried to pull myself together. As soon as Will's words registered in my brain, I jumped out of bed and quickly tiptoed down the stairs. Will was glued to the computer by the time I made it to the living room. Our church had sent out an email requesting prayers for Randy and Marilyn. They had flown to Idaho a few days earlier to visit their daughter, son-in-law, and grandchildren. While he was helping decorate for Christmas, Randy had suffered a heart attack.

Just three weeks prior, Randy and Marilyn had sat at our kitchen table. After poring over our finances, Randy asked, "Can we pray for you?" The girls played quietly near our newly-decorated tree as the four of us joined hands around our Craigslist table. "Lord, bless this family," Randy prayed. "Give them wisdom with their finances. Show them that you will provide for all their needs. Use this season of hardship for your glory."

By the time I pulled up a chair to huddle in front of the computer with Will, waiting for more news, a second email arrived.

Randy had passed away.

Why, God? Why?! I pleaded silently. *Right before Christmas? I know you are good, Lord. But there is nothing good about this.*

I choked on my tears as I said Marilyn's name out loud, over and over. "Poor Marilyn! Oh, Lord! Why take Randy from Marilyn?"

Back in my bed, I slept fitfully. Randy's death took me back to my college years, as I thought about my friend Courtney and how she had also died suddenly just before Christmas.

A week later, we stood hand in hand in a sanctuary brimming with Randy's loved ones—Marilyn, his three daughters and their spouses, grandchildren, extended family, and faraway friends who had traveled to be by his family's side. We worshipped together in celebration of Randy's life. Marilyn spoke of the godly way Randy had led their home. His daughters spoke of the Christlike example he had set for them. As they spoke, I touched my belly. No one but Marilyn and Randy knew we were expecting another baby. While people would probably expect use to wish for a boy since we already had two girls, I wondered if the Lord would give us a third daughter so we could be like Randy's family. I've seen Will cry only a handful of times in our twelve years of marriage, but neither of us could hold back the flood of tears that flowed that day. Through sobs, we ushered Randy into eternity with the song "In Christ Alone."

We felt hopeless. We were living in a financial drought. Yet three weeks before his death, Randy had given us hope that this stormy season would pass. God loved us and had a plan for us. If we trusted in His peace, our fears would still. If we would stop fighting the course and follow His direction, He would show us His provision.

We had navigated our marriage and family on ground that was shaky at best for the past few years. As we drove away from Randy's memorial service, Will reached over to where I sat and laced his fingers through mine before we even left the parking lot. With tears still in his eyes, he choked out: "I don't want to continue fighting, Erin. I want to be a husband and a father like Randy was. I want to lead our family well."

"And that you can," I squeeze his hand tightly. "You can."

A NEW PERSPECTIVE

JANUARY 2012

I opened the refrigerator and pantry and started making a mental menu plan. It wasn't that hard: Although the shelves were mostly bare, there were WIC tortillas and cheese and a can of black beans. Quesadillas, coming right up!

While we didn't have many options when it came to meals, we didn't go hungry. God met every need, and Randy's final, hope-filled words to us in the kitchen that day echoed in our ears. Still, times were hard. I vacillated between joy and fear or frustration. More than once, I leaned over the kitchen sink and held back tears because I didn't know how we would make it to the end of the month when Will got paid. It was then that the Lord spoke to me softly: *I will provide for all of your needs.*

What could we do? We had seen the Lord provide for us through government resources, donations from friends and strangers, and a few odd jobs. But it didn't seem like we were getting very far. Month after month, we still struggled. We barely had enough food to eat, and I was expecting our third child.

My mind went to Randy's words: "You don't have enough money. You have an income problem."

His words lit a fire under me. Already, Will and I were both working a variety of jobs, but none of them added up to enough. Besides barely covering our basic needs—even with the help of WIC and Medicaid—our mortgage on the house in Mississippi was now underwater. Its market value had plummeted; we owed more than it was worth. Our renters had moved out, and we were draining our meager savings to pay the mortgage on the house each month while we continued to pay rent on our townhouse. Soon our savings would run out. It was an impossible situation.

I looked at the silver platters displayed proudly above our kitchen cabinets. They had been wedding gifts, a mainstay among Southern matrons in small-town Mississippi. I thought about my sixteen place settings of fine china—also wedding gifts. I twirled the one-carat diamond on my finger; it was the most valuable item we owned. *Should we sell any of this? All of it? What else can we do?*

I started crying, thinking about how sad I would be to no longer have my ring and all those beautiful wedding presents. They were some of the only tangible items left from our former life—a life of prosperity wherein we didn't realize how prosperous we were.

Within minutes, though, the Holy Spirit inspired me to stop my internal pity party. While serving in Costa Rica for a year and traveling to places like China, Zimbabwe, and Peru on mission trips, Will and I had made friends with many believers in other countries. Some of their "upper" or "middle" classes lived at a level we would consider very simple. I felt ashamed. Any of our friends from overseas would walk into our kitchen and think we were rich because compared to most of the world, we were. I would be embarrassed for them to see our spacious townhome—so modest by American standards but enormous to many of them—and our superficial silver pieces and fine china displayed for all to see. Even in this moment, when I was feeling like we were groveling at the bottom, we were materially wealthy compared to the rest of the world. I prayed for wisdom and for some way for us to increase our income in a more substantial way, as Randy had suggested.

We never did sell our silver, china, or my ring, although we seriously considered it. They would have afforded us some short-term income, no doubt. But we needed to heed Randy's advice and explore options that would give us long-term financial stability.

THE HOME WE COULDN'T SELL

A month before Randy passed away, the tenant at our rental house in Mississippi broke his lease. One day he was there; the next he was gone. At that point, we had been trying to sell the house for nearly four years and were renting it out to make the mortgage payments. During those four years, the house had no more than four showings. The value had decreased to less than half of what we still owed on it. With the renter gone, we listed the home once again.

The house dangled on the market for months with no bites. At one point I asked our realtor, "Can we just foreclose on the house? We just want this burden gone." She suggested we call the bank. When I did, they told me foreclosure was not an option because we had never missed or even been late on a payment. So we continued to pay out of our small savings account. Finally, we got a short sale offer on the house. Although a short sale would affect our credit, it was better than a foreclosure, and it would allow us to sell the home for less than we owed. It sounded like a win-win. The meager offer didn't phase me; we wanted to be rid of the hardship, of the stress.

We were visiting Will's family in Mississippi when the papers came through. We excitedly filled them out, signing our names and checking boxes. One of the last questions on the form was "Have you ever rented out the property?" This question struck me as odd, and a strange, sinking feeling entered my stomach as I checked "yes." I had no idea why at the time.

Within days, the bank rejected the offer. Because of that final question, they categorized the house as an investment property, even though it was never an investment for us. As I mentioned in chapter 14, our loan had indicated we couldn't use the home for investment purposes. We hadn't read the fine print back in 2006 when we purchased it, and we never dreamed that renting it out in order to make our mortgage payments would result in not being able to sell it.

God provided another financial counselor just when we needed one. Barry Myers, a financial planning coach, was the husband of my blogger friend Stacy of humoroushomemaking .com. Stacy knew of our financial troubles, and she suggested they drive a few hours from their Virginia home to spend the weekend with us. We didn't have a guest room, but they had no qualms about sleeping on an air mattress on our living room floor. While our children played and Stacy and I chatted, Barry and Will pored over our finances. Like Randy, Barry said we didn't have a spending problem but an income problem. Barry suggested we talk to our bank and a lawyer about our options.

The bank told us they couldn't foreclose on the house until we stopped making payments. As long as we had money—any money—in our savings account, we didn't feel that was an ethical option. So we continued draining our account each month until our funds were gone. Then, and only then, did we proceed. We reserved enough money to pay a bankruptcy attorney from my parents' church. We then stopped making payments on the mortgage. Within weeks, the bank began calling me—and only me. My name was the only one on the loan, a decision we had made when we were trying to qualify based only on my salary, in an attempt to make "wise" financial choices and "live below our means." Because of this, the bank wouldn't talk to Will. I was under extreme stress, staying up most of the night trying to build an online business, and I was now seven months pregnant with our third daughter. Sometimes, the bank would call after 10:00 p.m. I began experiencing heart palpitations every time the phone rang. I worried that my anxiety would harm our unborn baby.

We never dreamed we would face bankruptcy, but we had gotten to the point where the bank gave us few options: We could either sell the home for what we still owed (which was impossible with the house being underwater), we could pay what we owed outright (which was impossible at our income level), or the bank could seize the home and possibly sue me. The only protection against being sued was for me to declare bankruptcy.

BANKRUPTCY COURT

The attorney's office was smack in the middle of the small town that housed my childhood church, the town where I had hidden in shame while applying for food stamps. Will and I dropped the girls off at my parents' house and drove to meet with the attorney. *Would he remember me from when I was a child? Would he recognize me as Bob and Becky's daughter?*

As I climbed the creaking steps in the old brick building, I prayed for peace and hoped my face wouldn't redden when the secretary ushered us into the office. The attorney smiled as we entered, shook our hands, and told us to take seats in front of his desk. He settled in his leather armchair and asked why we had come.

"We own a house in another state that we've been unable to sell," I began. "Will is a teacher at the high school, and we don't make enough money to cover all of our expenses, much less the house in Mississippi. We've drained our savings, and now the bank is proceeding with foreclosure. Someone suggested I declare bankruptcy to protect my assets."

The only "assets" we owned at this point were those silver platters, our china, and my engagement ring.

"Did you bring all of your debt notes with you?" the attorney asked.

We were puzzled. "What debt notes?" Will asked. "We have our mortgage statement. That is the only debt we have."

The attorney look surprised. "This is it?" he asked incredulously. "This is the *entirety* of your debt? Your house note?"

It seemed like no small sum to us, but we assured him we had no more debt. We hadn't used credit cards since we were married; we had no student loans and no medical bills. We simply had an overwhelming mortgage and no hope of paying it off.

"This is very rare that you have no other debt," the attorney mused. "Well, you definitely don't have a spending problem. But it does sound like you have an income problem. Declaring bankruptcy is nothing to consider lightly, but it will protect you from being sued after the bank repossesses the house. Especially with the mortgage being in Erin's name only, you need the protection."

"We do have a few assets," I began. "We have some silver platters, china . . ." I looked down at my fingers. "And my ring. Oh! And we just finished purchasing my parents' old minivan. It's officially in our name now. Should we try selling all that?"

The attorney shook his head. "That won't put a dent in this house note. And at your income level, you won't be able to pay this off for decades."

He then did something completely unexpected. He pulled out a Bible and opened to Deuteronomy 15. The passage chronicles God's command to the Israelites to cancel debts at the end of every seven years. The attorney went on to explain that many people believed the Founding Fathers of the United States had based bankruptcy law on this passage of Scripture. The men who founded our country made a way for those who were crippled by debt to be set free, he explained, just as God arranged for the Israelites to be freed of the debts they couldn't pay.

I had been a Christian for more than two decades, but I had never contemplated this Scripture. I had no prior knowledge of bankruptcy or the cancellation of debts. *Could God use even* this *humbling moment as further affirmation of His love for us, regardless of our mistakes?* In the end, we filed the bankruptcy papers, and by July of that year, we had a court date. We left the girls with my parents and drove to the courthouse an hour away. I was eight months pregnant. My sister had loaned me a dress to wear for Randy and Marilyn's youngest daughter's wedding a month prior, and now I wore the same navy blue sleeveless dress with silver sequins to bankruptcy court. I ironed an oxford shirt and suit pants for Will the night before, and he completed his outfit with a tie. We wanted to look presentable and dignified, even though we felt anything but.

We parked our minivan on the street in front of the courthouse. *Would anyone notice us?* I hoped not. We entered the old brick building and rode a musty elevator to the floor that housed the courtroom. We waited in the hallway on what looked like an old church pew. Someone finally opened the door, and we walked in with others who were there to declare bankruptcy. Technically, I was the one declaring bankruptcy since Will's name wasn't on the loan. I vacillated between relief that he was at my side and bitterness that even though we had made these financial choices together, *I* was the one paying for every single mistake. It was *my* credit that would be ruined. Here I was again—the model daughter, the overachieving student—with my pride toppling like a stack of Jenga blocks.

I crossed and uncrossed my legs as we waited. I held my belly. Our third daughter kicked and squirmed and reminded me of her presence as we awaited our fate. Would the judge free us from this burden? Either way, I felt ashamed. It wasn't *right* to declare bankruptcy. Just like it hadn't been *right* to use government aid. *Good Christian girls don't succumb to such lowly desperate measures,* I had told myself. But in that moment, we had no other choice.

As we waited, we listened to story after story of boats and vacation homes and credit card bills and all kinds of debt that other defendants were asking the judge to forgive. And, in almost every instant, he forgave them with a strike of his gavel. After waiting for what seemed like an eternity, he called my name.

Will and I rose. I waddled toward the front of the room, clearly due to give birth any day. Our attorney met us at the judge's desk. "Take a seat," the judge ordered. "And what debts do you seek forgiven?"

Our attorney took out a green khaki folder and pulled out some paperwork, with our house note front and center.

"Hmmmm," pondered the judge, as he glanced over the papers and examined the note more intently. "And what else?"

"This is it," our attorney responded. "It's just the mortgage."

"Very well," the judge swung the gavel onto his block.

It was finished.

FORGIVEN AND FREE

Will and I shook hands with our attorney, thanked him, and walked out of the courtroom. An unexpected sentiment filled me as soon as we hit the elevator: relief. On the ride home, I tried explaining the emotions welling inside of me to Will.

"Honey," I said, "I didn't realize how heavy this burden had weighed on me until just now. I feel light. I feel free." Moments before I had been weighed down with the millstone of the home we couldn't sell. Now the worst-case scenario of homeownership had happened to us, but I was overwhelmed with an inexplicable peace that we were going to be OK. Cars and trucks whizzed by as we drove down Interstate 77, but I was in another world. Tears streamed down my cheeks as I realized the heaviness that had lifted was no comparison to the weight of the debts of our sins that Jesus had paid for on the cross.

Matthew 11:28–30 became a reality for me that day: "Come to me, all you who are weary and burdened, and I will give you rest. Take my yoke upon you and learn from me, for I am gentle and humble in heart, and you will find rest for your souls. For my yoke is easy and my burden is light."

"Thank you, Jesus," I whispered. "Thank you, Lord."

SHOULD YOU DECLARE BANKRUPTCY?

Our story is one of forgiveness, redemption, and grace. But would I declare bankruptcy all over again if I had the choice? The answer is difficult. I believe bankruptcy should be a last-ditch effort to salvage one's finances. We were living on a low income with no relief in sight. Without the protection of bankruptcy, I would've personally had to live with the threat of lawsuits from the bank hanging over my head. We had no other debts, but the mortgage was an extremely weighty one.

"The problem with bankruptcy is that it is the government who is saying that you are off the hook with your bills," wrote SeedTime.com blogger Bob Lotich in a post titled "Bankruptcy and the Bible."[1] "In most cases the businesses that you owe money to probably would still like to collect payment. It is actually doing a great disservice to the companies that you owe money to. Essentially, the borrower/buyer made a promise to pay, but is allowed (via bankruptcy) to break the agreement."

In his post, Bob quotes Psalm 37:21, "The wicked borrow and do not repay, but the righteous give generously" and Ecclesiastes 5:5, "It is better not to make a vow than to make one and not fulfill it."

Although my credit score is now much better, the bankruptcy is still on my record. As much as I combatted anger toward Will because he would make it through that trial without the mark of bankruptcy on his name as well, it was a grace in disguise. We didn't plan it, but because his credit remained intact, we were able to purchase a home one year after I declared bankruptcy. This would have been impossible if the home loan on the house in Mississippi had been in both of our names. Still, if I were to apply for a job or loan today, potential employees and creditors would see this embarrassing part of my past. Did declaring bankruptcy lift a burden for me? Yes. Would I do it again if I had *any* other way out? No. I still believe bankruptcy should be avoided at all costs and only used as a last resort.

HE RESTORES

I will restore to you the years that the swarming locust has eaten.

JOEL 2:25 ESV

Living on a low income and the humility of surviving on government aid, losing our home, and declaring bankruptcy built our faith like never before. It's easy to trust God when you feel like your needs are met; it's a different story when you have to trust Him to meet every single need. During this time we clung to the promise of His restoration, and to the promise that He would use our story—as difficult as it was to live—to somehow impact others and turn their hearts toward Him.

You, too, dear reader, can embrace the hope of rising above your circumstances, even when they are as bleak as ours were. You can pick up the pieces of humbling times and see fruit in the aftermath—relationships restored, burdens lifted, and a heart of positivity that blooms and grows.

SIXTEEN

WHEN THE TUNNEL'S STILL DARK

In the middle of the night God will often sing songs to you like the nightingale that you'd never hear in the day time, and He means for you to hear them and sing them to others in the morning.

GEORGE MATHESON

AUGUST 2012

We were still struggling financially when our third daughter was born, but a light had finally dawned at the end of the tunnel we had been stuck in for years. Will started teaching at a different school, and the position came with a pay raise. I had also started generating income on my website, thehumbledhomemaker. com. We never dreamed that within a year of our daughter's birth, we would be making enough money to go from barely surviving to thriving.

The money I made blogging grew slowly but steadily. I never set out to replace Will's income; I simply wanted to help make ends meet. My impossible dream at the time was to eventually send our children to a Christian school. Even at a fraction of the cost of other academies, it would still be difficult without a scholarship. I had written about the school for the local newspaper when our oldest was two. *Oh, Lord,* I prayed, *if only I can make enough money on the blog over the course of the next four years, so we can send our little girl to kindergarten at that school . . . I know how to survive on a low income; we can continue to cut corners any way possible—if only we can send her to that school.* It sounds almost ludicrous now; we could barely afford to feed our family, yet I dreamed of giving our children a Christian education like the one my parents had given me.

I distinctively remember the day I calculated how much money I had been making as a blogger. Before, it was mere pocket change, so I hadn't kept a faithful accounting. But as our bank account fattened, it became obvious that our situation was turning around. As soon as I saw that our income exceeded qualifications for the year, I called the Department of Social Services to cancel our assistance. My heart drummed rapidly as I nervously dialed the number. Government benefits had been a lifeblood to us during this period of financial challenges. *Would we really be OK without them? What if our income fell drastically again? What if we couldn't make it on our own?* But I knew it was the right thing to do. Just as God provided for us through our WIC checks and Medicaid, He would meet all of our needs without them as well.

"Hi! This is Erin Odom. I need to cancel our WIC and Medicaid, please."

"It's OK," the receptionist said. "It looks like you don't need to re-qualify for another six months. You should be able to keep your benefits through the end of the year."

"No," I insisted. "We are overqualified now. We no longer meet the requirements. Please take us off."

The lady on the other end of the line finally agreed to remove us from the system, and I breathed a sigh of relief. With bankruptcy months behind us, a new job for Will, and the blog taking off as a business, I felt we were finally starting to make progress. Randy and Barry had been right: there *was* hope.

A NEW HOME

By continuing to live frugally, and with Will's pay raise, we saved most of my earnings that year. When our landlord called to tell us he was selling the townhouse, it opened up the door for us to begin looking for a home of our own. Instead of relying on what the bank told us we could afford, we based our home search solely on Will's teacher income. By living below our means, we were able to put enough money down on our home to avoid PMI and ensure a reasonable monthly payment. As soon as we saw our future home for sale, we had a feeling it was for us.

Later, we discovered the owners were selling the house before departing to Africa to be missionaries. We'd never been able to sell our house in Mississippi when we dreamed of leaving for the mission field—and we never arrived in Mexico. Now, somehow, it felt like buying this house was redeeming that loss for us. We were coming full circle and helping another family accomplish what we hadn't been able to achieve.

The house was perfect for our growing family: four bedrooms, two and a half baths, and just over 2,000 square feet in an older, quiet subdivision. The owners even threw in a backyard playset for the girls. After moving in, I asked the Lord if we were selling out—after all, it had been my nightmare to settle in the suburbs. I thought of the opportunities we'd lost during our time in the townhouse. We were so consumed by financial crises during those years that we neglected to embrace what could have been a time of encouragement to our neighbors. I thought back to the widow across the street, the single dad next door, and immigrant families with whom we shared that little subdivision. We occasionally shared meals and spoke to each other while out on family walks, but was it enough? What opportunities did we miss to further reflect the gospel to these families because we were so engulfed in our own struggles?

Those four years in the townhouse were hard. I'd grappled with pregnancy and depression and trials and sometimes wondering how in the world we'd be able to afford to eat. I spent so much time wrapped up in my own world that I let people pass me by. I prayed to remember the good from that season, leave behind the bad, and live more intentionally in our new home, in our new neighborhood.

But, God, I whispered, *did you really call us to be missionaries? Will we ever be back serving people internationally again?*

He reminded me how I'd wrestled with my calling in college, of a late-night battle in the student newspaper office where 22-year-old Erin told God she didn't want to just *write*, that she wanted to *live* in Latin America, to truly *see* the impact she was making for the kingdom.

Erin, you will reach more people through writing, I felt Him say. The words were not audible but a distinct calling no less. *You will reach more people through writing.*

I had no idea blogs existed back in 2003. I had added Spanish as a second major, and, by golly, I wanted to use it. I did *not* want to be stuck behind a computer screen writing my life away. Surely I would reach more people face-to-face than via a small newspaper or magazine. And a book? I would never dare face the rejection of "real" book publishing.

A decade later, writing became a tool God used to rescue us from our cycle of low-income living, one blog post at a time. Gradually, Will and I began working together on the blogging business, and in late 2016 he resigned from his teaching job so we could both work on the blog full-time, all while raising our four children at home. Now here I am publishing a book—a book chronicling our journey of low-income living and God's provision and hand throughout. Writing has become the conduit through which God is fulfilling His missionary calling on my life.

So we bought that house. We put $30,000 down on the 2,000-square-foot home in the suburbs, and I prayed, *Yes, God, I'll write. But please, God, help me not to forget. Help me not to settle. Help me practice gratitude every day.*

For the first year we lived in our home, not a day went by that I didn't pull our minivan into the driveway, turn off the engine, rest my arms on the steering wheel, look up at the house, and thank God for it. Sometimes the girls would ask me, "Mommy, why aren't we getting out of the car?"

"I'm just admiring all that God has provided, sweethearts," I'd say. "Isn't God so good? He gave us this house, girls. He has provided for all of our needs."

Today, much of our life still looks the same. Even though we have more income, we don't have cable television or fancy home furnishings. I still shop clearance and consignment; I still embrace hand-me-downs, and discount stores are my jam. This frugality has allowed us to achieve that "impossible" dream of sending our children to Christian school. I cried tears of thanksgiving when I dropped our oldest off there on her first day of kindergarten. Those tears come back every year.

Our life is far from perfect. We sometimes still squabble about money. We're still learning to redirect our thoughts to trust rather than anxiety that we'll have enough. Will, the most generous person I know, has to remind me on a regular basis, "We're not still living on a low income. We can give more now. We can bless others with what the Lord has blessed us with."

Exiting financial frustration is a process—one we have to cultivate. It would be very easy to fall back into the kinds of unwise choices we made in our newlywed years, and we hold God's provision for today with an open hand. We're both keenly aware that it wasn't me who turned around our financial situation. Nor was it Will. It was God, friends. It was God. He was there—leading us, opening some doors and closing others, and teaching us to depend only on Him, every single step of the way.

IS YOUR TUNNEL STILL DARK?

I clearly remember when there seemed to be no light at the end of the tunnel. I thought life would never get better. We would never be able to breathe. And we would always be barely making it.

I hope I never forget our time in that dark tunnel of financial frustration. Yet even then, our challenges didn't scratch the surface of what many people experience. I know that our life would still have been considered "rich" by the standards of the people we had served in developing countries, even though by American standards we were "poor."

I pray I never forget the way my cheeks burned as I pulled out my WIC checks to pay for groceries. Should I have felt ashamed? No. But I had witnessed the judgment of those who accept help, and it tormented me.

I don't want to forget that the only way I attended women's events at church was via scholarships—scholarships I was too embarrassed to apply for in person.

I hope I never forget how the telephone calls about our mortgage bill bred deep anxiety during my third pregnancy. Despite our best efforts, the scars of foreclosure and bankruptcy will always haunt me—but they don't have to define me.

The crazy thing is, I'm thankful I lived all this.

The humility of our season of financial frustration brought me face-to-face with real need, and real *provision*. More than anything, our time in the tunnel tuned our hearts to God's. We failed to acknowledge or appreciate the Lord's provision when it seemed we were meeting all of our own needs, when we had enough money for excess. But when every penny counted, when our budget never made sense on paper, when we had cents instead of dollars in our bank account at the end of the month, *that* was when we learned that only God is the provider of all of our needs.

Are you there now, friend? You don't see a way out. Hope is dim. There is no light. Are you stumbling around in the fog? Is the tunnel still dark?

My greatest hope, dear reader, is that my story has encouraged you that your situation isn't hopeless. No, your story won't look exactly like mine or the others you met in these pages. Each family and financial situation is unique. But my prayer is that although you might not *see* God's hand in your life right now, you now realize that He is right there with you. Ask Him for wisdom. Pray for the ability to recognize His provision. Surrender your life to *His* plan, not to what the world deems success.

Do you have a spending problem? You don't have to be a slave to your spending habits. Jesus can set you free from the bondage of excessive spending. The first step is admitting you have a problem and asking Him for help.

Do you have an income problem? Ask the Lord to reveal ways you can increase your income. Do you need to change careers or start a business? My prayer is that this book has given you some ideas on how to work toward exiting the low-income life while not being ashamed to seek the help you need to provide for your family's needs in the meantime.

In John 16:33 Jesus says, "In this world you will have trouble. But take heart! I have overcome the world." God doesn't promise us a life of health, wealth, and prosperity, but He does promise to provide exactly what we need, when we need it. With the right attitude and perspective, we can look back on a season of economic challenge as some of the most faith-building days of our lives. It was for our family, and it can be for yours, too.

I have no doubt that exiting the tunnel of financial frustration can be an exciting reality for you. I hope that by working hard and implementing some of the tips in this book, you'll find yourself on your way to the financial freedom you've been longing for, even if the tunnel is still a dark place for you right now.

I can't give you a one-size-fits-all formula to make it right again. But what I can do is point you in the direction of the One who planned your life before time began. Take heart and have hope, my friend: Jesus is waiting for you on the other side of the tunnel, and He will meet you in the middle of it. He will walk through it with you, and He will be the light at the end of it as well.

I began this chapter with a quote from the Scottish minister and hymn writer George Matheson:

In the middle of the night God will often sing songs to you like the nightingale that you'd never hear in the day time, and He means for you to hear them and sing them to others in the morning.

When we were just barely making it, I prayed that God would somehow use our challenges to encourage others one day. It was a dark season of our lives, yet God "sang" to us in that season in ways we wouldn't have been able to hear otherwise. He taught us to trust Him to meet our daily needs. He showed us over and over again that He alone is the Great Provider. And He put people in our path—Randy and Marilyn, Barry and Stacy, Marnie, and so many others—who helped us to move from barely surviving to more than just making it. This book has been our song in the morning, to encourage you in what might still be your nighttime. My prayer is that the songs you are hearing now will become morning songs for you one day as well—that you will encourage others with your own story of moving from financial frustration to hope.

Because there is hope, dear friend. There is hope.

ACKNOWLEDGMENTS

When I was living the story of this book, I told myself that I would write about it one day—and do all I could to change the shame and the stigma of the poor. I also wanted to take what we had learned and give the practical tips that anyone could apply to their lives, no matter the income level or season of financial well-being.

Without the following people, that dream would have remained an idea in my head.

My Lord and Savior Jesus: You were there all along, leading us, sustaining us, calling us to Yourself and making a way for us to point others to You as well. You are the great redeemer and the restorer of the years the locusts ate.

Will: We lived this story together. It wasn't glamorous, and at times it was downright grueling—but God had a plan all along. Thank you for believing in me and in the message of this book enough to take over homeschool days and cook innumerable meals so I could write, send me away on writing retreats, and simply be the best husband and daddy. I love you.

My three girls: You are the reason I started the blog—in hopes of making a better way for you. You, your brother, and your daddy are the most important part of my life. I love you more than rainbows, and to the moon and back.

Baby Boy: You were the best surprise during the writing of this book. We wrote it together. Baby Boy, you're a joy to me.

Mama: The day you marched into my first-grade classroom with your dictionary in hand is forever etched in my memory. I had written a story about a giraffe reaching into the trees to eat the luscious leaves, and when the teacher wrote that "luscious" wasn't a word, you proved her wrong—and ignited in me a love for writing. Thank you for being my first and greatest editor. Those late nights spent poring over term papers weren't wasted.

Daddy: You taught me that a hard work ethic pays off, and that God and family matter so much more than money. Thank you and Mama both for focusing our family on the eternal.

TO THOSE WHO WALKED WITH US THROUGH THIS STORY:

Marilyn: God used you and Randy to change the whole trajectory of our story. Randy made an impact until the end. He finished the race strong and I am confident he is now reaping the reward of a life well lived in the presence of our Savior.

The Myers: Thank you for your constant encouragement and belief that we could turn our financial situation around, even when all hope seemed lost.

Holly: Thank you for being my sounding board, my mentor, and one of my dearest friends—and for entertaining the baby during a long but incredibly fun day of filming.

Brantley: Not only were you the best college roommate, but you were the first person to suggest I start a blog. Without that blog, there would be no book.

Beth M.: Your prayers from a world away have not gone

unheard. Thank you for pleading with the Father on our behalf during our darkest moments.

The Taylors, St. Clairs, and Rosses: Thank you for being some of the best friends we could ask for—for loving us in and through our struggles, in want and in plenty.

Teague C-Group and my church family: Thank you for praying me through this project.

TO THOSE WHO MADE THIS BOOK A REALITY:

Bill: You took a chance on a random blogger when you sent me that first email back in January 2014. Thank you for following the Lord's leading and for believing in me when I didn't believe in myself. Without you, this book would not be.

Lindsay: Thank you for being the best launch team manager ever! I couldn't have done it without you.

Crystal: Thank you for your savvy business mentoring, but more than that, thank you for being a dear friend.

My mastermind groups—the Christian Authors, the Excellence Mastermind, and the Green Ninjas: Thank you for the feedback, encouragement, and prayers. You know who you are.

Megan T., Beth R., Elsie, Kelly S., and Dawn M.: Thank you for reading my book in its roughest form, offering me feedback, and most of all encouraging me that the world needed this story.

Amy: You're the best makeup artist ever. The Lord has given you a gift to enhance natural beauty. I was nervous for someone else to do my makeup for the book's trailer. But girl, you nailed it.

Katherine and Shauna: Thank you for proofreading this manuscript and making sure it was clear of random typos and misplaced commas.

Families I interviewed: Thank you for trusting me with your stories—and for being willing to let me share them with the world who needed to hear them.

TO MY TEAM AT ZONDERVAN:

I remember tracing my fingers over the big "Z" in the NIV Student Bible my parents gave me for high school graduation. I rarely noticed the publisher of most books I read, but for some reason, I always took note of Zondervan. Perhaps now I know why.

Carolyn: I wanted to work with you from the moment I met you at Allume 2014. I told Bill right away how much I loved you. He said: "Everyone loves Carolyn." He was right. Thank you for taking a chance on me and for believing in and preserving the heart of my story. I'm so grateful for you.

Stephanie and Harmony: You ladies ROCK. Truly. You both work word magic. Stephanie, you are a saint for working with me through cuts when I went half a book over word count *and* for exercising an incredible amount of patience when I had a baby the week of a major deadline. Your suggestions were solid and made this book so much better. Harmony, your encouragement gave me the confidence I was lacking. You helped make this book complete. Thank you both for being my biggest cheerleaders and for believing in me and this message. I hope we can meet in person one day. I think we will laugh over coffee, for I feel we are already friends.

Ben: The day you filmed our family is one of my favorite memories from this book. You were encouraging, patient, and made the day so much fun. What a blessing you are to so many authors.

Alicia: Thank you for working your marketing mojo. You brought so much energy to this project! Tom, thank you for putting Alicia on my team. You are both such a blessing.

Jennifer: Thank you for all your work in getting publicity for this book.

Bridgette: Thanks for making sure I had all my endorsements.

The Sales Team: I don't know your names, but I know you are AMAZING! You got my book into Target and so many other venues! Seriously—you are awesome. Thank you!

David: Thank you for the opportunity to publish a book with Zondervan. It's a dream come true—a dream I was afraid to say aloud until it happened.

To all of you, I am forever grateful.

NOTES

CHAPTER 1: When Your Economy Crumbles

1. Diane Whitmore Schanzenbach et al., "The Great Recession: Over but Not Gone?" Northwestern University Institute for Policy Research, February 2014, http://www.ipr.northwestern.edu/about/news/2014/IPR-research-Great-Recession-unemployment-foreclosures-safety-net-fertility-public-opinion.html
2. Lisa Leake, "Budget Day 1: Getting Organized," 100 Days of Real Food, October 5, 2010, http://www.100daysofrealfood.com/2010/10/05/budget-day-1-getting-organized/.

CHAPTER 2: And It All Comes Tumbling Down

1. "Chart Book: The Legacy of the Great Recession," Center on Budget and Policy Priorities, last modified June 9, 2017, http://www.cbpp.org/research/economy/chart-book-the-legacy-of-the-great-recession?fa=view&id=3252.
2. "Great Recession," Wikipedia, last modified January 1, 2017, http://en.wikipedia.org/wiki/Great_Recession.
3. Diane Whitmore Schanzenbach et al., "The Great Recession: Over But Not Gone?," Northwestern University Institute for Policy Research, February 2014, http://www.ipr.northwestern.edu/about/news/2014/IPR-research-Great-Recession-unemployment-foreclosures-safety-net-fertility-public-opinion.html.
4. Hilary W. Hoynes et al., "Understanding Food Insecurity During the Great Recession," *Recession Trends*, October 2012, http://web.stanford.edu/group/recessiontrends/cgi-bin/web/resources/

research-project/understanding-food-insecurity-during-great
-recession.

5. Jad Mouawad, "Gas Prices Soar, Posing a Threat to Family
Budget," *New York Times*, February 27, 2008, http://www.nytimes
.com/2008/02/27/business/27gas.html?_r=0.

6. Marco Del Negro et al., "Why Didn't Inflation Collapse in the
Great Recession?," *Liberty Street Economics,* August 13, 2014,
http://libertystreeteconomics.newyorkfed.org/2014/08/why-didnt
-inflation-collapse-in-the-great-recession.html.

7. "The Precarious State of Family Balance Sheets," The Pew
Charitable Trust, last modified February 5, 2016, http://www
.pewtrusts.org/en/research-and-analysis/reports/2015/01/the
-precarious-state-of-family-balance-sheets.

8. Neil Shah, "For Many U.S. Families, Financial Disaster Is Just
One Setback Away," *The Wall Street Journal*, January 29, 2015,
http://blogs.wsj.com/economics/2015/01/29/for-many-u-s-families
-financial-disaster-is-just-one-setback-away/.

9. Brian Wingfield, "The End of the Great Recession? Hardly,"
Forbes, September 20, 2010, http://www.forbes.com/sites/
brianwingfield/2010/09/20/the-end-of-the-great-recession
-hardly/#60a5e09d276b.

CHAPTER 3: When You Can Barely Make Ends Meet

1. "Who Are the Working Poor in America?" Center for Poverty
Research, http://poverty.ucdavis.edu/faq/who-are-working-poor.

2. Karen Weese, "'Hi, I'm Right Here': An Open Letter to Paul Ryan
about Poverty and Empathy," Salon, March 10, 2014, http://www
.salon.com/2014/03/10/hi_im_right_here_an_open_letter_to_paul
_ryan_about_poverty_and_empathy/.

3. Beth Ricci, "Dear Middle Class America, I Have a Bone to Pick
with You," Red and Honey, June 9, 2012, http://redandhoney.com/
dear-middle-class-america-i-have-a-bone-to-pick-with-you/.

4. Lauren Greutman, "5 Things I Learned As a Recovering Spender,"
Lauren Greutman, http://www.laurengreutman.com/5-things-i
-learned-as-a-recovering-spender/.

5. Crystal Paine, "Do Not Give Up Ever!," Money Saving Mom,
January 12, 2012, http://moneysavingmom.com/2012/01/do-not
-give-up-ever.html.

CHAPTER 4: Curbing Spending

1. Suzanne Kearns, "The Psychology of Money: How Saving and Spending Habits Are Programmed in Your Brain," Money Crashers, http://www.moneycrashers.com/psychology-of-money-saving-spending-habits/.

2. Scott I. Rick et al., "Tightwads and Spendthrifts," *Journal of Consumer Research* 34 (2008), http://www-personal.umich.edu/~prestos/Consumption/pdfs/RickCryderLoewenstein2007.pdf.

3. Ibid.

4. "Bipolar Excessive Spending," Bipolar Lives, http://www.bipolar-lives.com/bipolar-excessive-spending.html.

5. John M. Kuzma and Donald W. Black, "Compulsive Shopping: When Spending Begins to Consume the Consumer," *Current Psychiatry* 5 (July 2006), http://www.mdedge.com/currentpsychiatry/article/62268/compulsive-shopping-when-spending-begins-consume-consumer.

6. Beth Moore, *Living Free: Learning to Pray God's Word* (Nashville: LifeWay Press, 2015).

7. Lauren Greutman, "Why I Can't Go to Target Alone," Lauren Greutman, http://www.laurengreutman.com/cant-go-target-alone/.

CHAPTER 5: Building Your Budget

1. NPR Staff and James Doubek, "Attention, Students: Put Your Laptops Away," NPR, April 17, 2016, http://www.npr.org/2016/04/17/474525392/attention-students-put-your-laptops-away.

2. Dave Ramsey, *The Total Money Makeover: A Proven Plan for Financial Fitness* (Nashville: Thomas Nelson, 2013).

3. Ibid.

CHAPTER 6: Eating Well on a Rice and Beans Budget

1. April D. Lewis, *The Beginner's Guide to Zero Waste Cooking* (April D. Lewis, 2015).

2. Tiffany Terczak, "Fresh Start Day 21: Go Meatless (and Save!)," Don't Waste the Crumbs, January 30, 2013, http://dontwastethecrumbs.com/2013/01/fresh-start-day-21-go-meatless-and-save/.

3. Anne Simpson, *Your Grocery Budget Toolbox* (Amazon Digital Services LLC, 2012).

CHAPTER 11: The Elephant in the Church: The Government
Aid Question

1. Donald Miller, *Blue Like Jazz* (Nashville: Thomas Nelson, 2003).
2. Medicaid, accessed September 8, 2016, http://www.medicaid.gov.
3. "North Carolina Food Stamp Program," Benefits.gov, accessed September 8, 2016, https://www.benefits.gov/benefits/benefit -details/1389.
4. "Frequently Asked Questions about WIC," United States Department of Agriculture Food and Nutrition Service, accessed September 8, 2016, http://www.fns.usda.gov/wic/frequently-asked-questions-about-wic#2.
5. "Applying for Free and Reduced Price School Meals," United States Department of Agriculture Food and Nutrition Service, accessed Sept. 9, 2016, http://www.fns.usda.gov/school-meals/applying-free -and-reduced-price-school-meals.
6. Tim Worstall, "Extended Unemployment Benefits Really Did Raise the Unemployment Rate; They Still Are," *Forbes*, January 31, 2015, http://www.forbes.com/sites/timworstall/2015/01/31/extended-unemployment-benefits-really-did-raise-the-unemployment-rate-they -still-are/#417694b7399e.
7. Merriam-Webster's Learner's Dictionary, S.V. "oppress," http:/www .learnersdictionary.com/definition/oppress.

CHAPTER 12: Changing Our Mindsets

1. Richard Beck, *The Slavery of Death* (Eugene: Cascade Books, 2013).
2. Ibid.

CHAPTER 14: Redefining the American Dream

1. "American Dream," Wikipedia, last modified December 30, 2016, http://en.wikipedia.org/wiki/American_Dream.
2. Jonathan Chew, "Half of Millennials Believe the American Dream Is Dead," *Fortune*, December 11, 2015, http://fortune.com/2015/ 12/11/american-dream-millennials-dead/.
3. Rakesh Kochhar et al., "The American Middle Class Is Losing Ground," Pew Research Center, December 9, 2015, http://www.pewsocialtrends .org/2015/12/09/the-american-middle-class-is-losing-ground/

4. Phil Ciciora, "Paper: Homeownership a 'Dream Deferred' for Millennial Generation," Illinois News Bureau, February 8, 2016, http://news.illinois.edu/blog/view/6367/323642.

5. Armahn Rassuli, "Immigrants Face Harsh Challenges in Search of American Dream," *Collegiate Times*, November 5, 2015, http://www.collegiatetimes.com/opinion/immigrants-face-harsh-challenges-in-search-of-american-dream/article_057be5f4–842a-11e5-b519-c7efd507791d.html.

6. Chris Hedges and Joe Sacco, *Days of Destruction, Days of Revolt* (New York: Nation Books, 2014)

7. "Keeping Up with the Joneses," Wikipedia, last modified November 22, 2016, http://en.wikipedia.org/wiki/Keeping_up_with_the_Joneses.

8. Marianne Cooper, "The Downsizing of the American Dream," *The Atlantic*, October 2, 2015, http://www.theatlantic.com/business/archive/2015/10/american-dreams/408535/.

9. Rachel Catriona Jonat, *The Minimalist Mom's Guide to Baby's First Year* (CreateSpace Independent Publishing Platform, 2011).

10. Ibid.

11. Ibid.

12. Crystal Paine, "31 Days of Giving on a Budget Series," Money Saving Mom, December 2012, http://moneysavingmom.com/series/31-days-of-giving-on-a-budget.

13. Crystal Paine, *Money Making Mom* (Nashville: Thomas Nelson, 2015).

14. Shane Ferro, "Why Millennials Are Shut Out Of The American Dream," The Huffington Post, February 12, 2016, http://www.huffingtonpost.com/entry/another-reminder-that-millennials-will probably-die-poor_us_56bce574e4b0c3c550507d95.

CHAPTER 15: Bankruptcy of the Heart

1. Bob Lotich, "Bankruptcy and the Bible," SeedTime, http://christianpf.com/bankruptcy-and-the-bible/.

MORE WISDOM FROM
ERIN ODOM

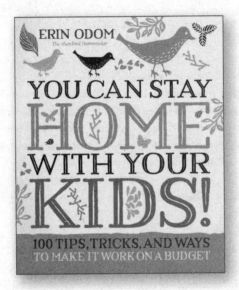

Investing your life in your family brings you joy, and doing it on a single income doesn't need to stress you out! Join Erin Odom as she shows you how you can live frugally—and thrive—while you raise your kids at home in *You Can Stay Home with Your Kids!*

Available April 2018